Understanding Toddler Development

Understanding
Toddler
Development

Margaret B. Puckett & Janet K. Black

with Joseph M. Moriarity

Redleaf Press
www.redleafpress.org
800-423-8309

Published by Redleaf Press
a division of Resources for Child Caring
10 Yorkton Court
St. Paul, MN 55117
Visit us online at www.redleafpress.org.

© 2007 by Redleaf Press. Adapted from *The Young Child*, © 2005, 2001, 1996, 1992 by Pearson Education, Inc., Upper Saddle River, NJ 07458.

First edition 2007
Cover photograph by Steve Wewerka
Interior typeset in Janson Text
Interior illustrations by Chris Wold Dyrud
Printed in Canada
14 13 12 11 10 09 08 07   1 2 3 4 5 6 7 8

Redleaf Press books are available at a special discount when purchased in bulk for special premiums and sales promotions. For details, contact the sales manager at 800-423-8309.

Library of Congress Cataloging-in-Publication Data
Puckett, Margaret B.
      Understanding toddler development / Margaret B. Puckett and Janet K. Black with Joseph M. Moriarity. -- 1st ed.
            p. cm.
      Includes bibliographical references and index.
      ISBN 978-1-933653-02-0
      1. Toddlers--Development. I. Black, Janet K. II. Moriarity, Joseph M. III. Title.
      HQ774.5.P83 2006
      305.231--dc22
                                    2006034665

Printed on acid-free paper.

Understanding Toddler Development

Introduction

Whether you are a parent or early childhood professional, you know that caring for and raising children are rewarding challenges: They represent the best of times and the worst of times—sometimes at virtually the same time!

Raising children in the United States has become even more difficult over the last few decades. Parents work more hours, commute farther, are more stressed, and have less free time now than ever before. The media and our consumer culture do not always act in the best interests of our children. Ads targeted directly at even very young children constantly promote unhealthy foods as well as toys and games of questionable value. Much of the entertainment that popular media offers is violent, even those shows supposedly designed for children, and more than a thousand studies have shown that movie and television violence fosters real violence.

And yet, more than ever before, parents and other caregivers have access to more accurate information about how children develop and how adults can support their growth and development. This knowledge is an important tool for those who interact with, care for, and provide educational experiences to infants and young children.

By the end of the first year, infants have taken huge steps in all areas of development: sensory, physical/motor, social, emotional, cognitive, and language. But the most obvious change parents and child care professionals see in infants is in their physical growth and the range of new motor skills they develop. Some of their first large-motor skills—pulling up, standing alone, and taking their first steps—generate excitement, praise, and celebration in their caregivers. These milestones are signs that a new period in child development has started—the *toddler period*. This period extends from age one through age two and into the third year.

This book is designed to be both a text on toddlers and a manual for working with toddlers. As you read and study this book and the other two books in this series—*Understanding Infant Development* and *Understanding Preschooler Development*—you'll learn much about our current knowledge of child development, including:

- the long-term effects of early biological and psychological experiences on brain growth and neurological development
- the influence of culture in many areas of growth and development
- how children learn
- important theories of child development
- how early life experiences can prepare children for reading
- how children learn cultural and moral values
- the effects of nurturing care on emotional development and stability in later life

You'll also discover that recent research has challenged many traditional theories on how best to support infant growth and development. At the same time, some of the old tried-and-true theories are still relevant today. What is important in the end is that the theories and current research presented here help parents and early childhood professionals improve the quality of life and education for the children under their care.

Part One

Physical and Motor Development

Little children are not logical—they are motor. To give children joy, give them something to do.

—Lucy Gage

In part 1, we will look closely at the remarkable three years of growth and development that make up the toddler period. During infancy, children are relatively helpless. Their ability to communicate with others and to explore their environment is extremely limited. But dramatic, remarkable, and exciting changes take place over the next three years. These changes and toddlers' growing abilities require that parents and other caregivers provide a more stimulating, yet safe, environment for the very motivated exploring and experimenting that toddlers will do.

In the following chapters, you'll learn what patterns of physical and motor development you can expect in children at this age, and you'll learn to identify the developmental landmarks in large- and small-muscle development. You'll look at factors that influence physical and motor development and learn more about creating an environment that supports and enhances that growth.

You'll also learn about the mutual relationship between physical/motor and sensory development at this age, called *perceptual-motor development*. Physical/motor development is greatly affected by the health and normal functioning of toddlers' senses, especially vision and hearing. At the same time, the development of toddlers' perceptions of space, depth, and weight depend greatly on locomotor experiences. Understanding and being able to identify developmental landmarks in perceptual-motor development will help you recognize problems in toddlers in your care.

Physical/motor and psychosocial development are also closely linked. You'll learn more about how new motor skills help build toddlers' growing body awareness and sense of self-worth. A toddler's early sense of self is based on their interactions with their parents, their caregivers, and other important adults in their lives. These relationships, together with toddlers' increasing sense of their own abilities, actually create the foundation for their emerging self-concepts. This is also the time when children become curious about gender and body parts and when caregivers can begin the process of toilet training.

Neurological development and brain growth are very rapid during the first three years of their lives. In this chapter, you'll explore the important relationship between physical/motor development and cognitive growth. You'll learn about factors that influence physical and motor development, such as nutrition, food preferences, and sleep patterns, and how these affect cognitive development.

Toddlers tend to act without thinking, have little experience, poor judgment, and great curiosity. These characteristics, together with their growing desire to be independent, put them at risk for accidents and injuries. Here, we'll offer suggestions and strategies to lessen those risks.

During the toddler years, the rapid growth of infancy, while somewhat slower in the second year, continues. As their bodies grow stronger and more coordinated, toddlers can more fully begin to explore the world around them. We begin in chapter 1 by looking more deeply at the fascinating connections between toddlers' culture and their growth, development, and learning.

1 Social and Cultural Influences on Development

Theories of Development

Children come into the world as seemingly blank slates, but in fact, the slate isn't completely blank. As anyone who has raised or cared for young children knows, their personalities differ from one another at a very early age—even from their siblings. By the time they're a year old, they are clearly their "own person" with likes and dislikes and rapidly growing, yet differing, abilities.

Child development researchers have long debated the question of personality: how much is inherited (nature) and how much is affected by how we are raised (nurture). They have created a number of theories about how growth happens, what causes us to behave in certain ways, and how and why we have some abilities and talents, but not others.

According to some researchers and child psychologists, growth and development are controlled mainly by heredity, that is, we are born with a kind of blueprint that defines what, when, and how much each aspect of growth and development will happen. This is called the *maturationist* theory of development.

Others believe that the environment in which we grow up plays a much more important role. According to this theory, called *behaviorism*, family life and culture affect the kind of adult we become much more than our genes.

Another theory, *developmental interaction*, takes a different view. It says that children are born with certain abilities that can blossom when supported by a rich and stimulating environment, or can be impaired by an environment lacking in mental stimulation and rewards.

Still others suggest a *transactional perspective* in which a person's inherited traits and environmental experiences affect each other through regular interactions between heredity and environment. Inherited traits are shaped by experience and experience is shaped by inherited traits.

Perhaps the most prominent theory of child growth, development, and learning today—the *systems approach*—proposes that a variety of influences affect who we become. They include biology, race, ethnicity, cultural and religious values, tradition, gender, financial status, and more.

Although humans are genetically programmed for coordination, movement, and mobility, environmental differences in early childhood mean that toddlers will begin developing various motor abilities at different times—throwing objects from a crib, standing alone, walking without falling, bending to pick up objects, and so on. Such differences are viewed as simply that—different, neither good nor bad, normal nor abnormal.

Social and Cultural Influences on Development

Despite physical and genetic differences, most toddlers reach the developmental milestones and goals needed to survive and take part in their own cultures. The many cultures on our planet have their own views about how children should be cared for and what they should be taught. Here are a few examples:

- In cultures where extended families are still more intact and family members depend on each other more for support and identity (such as in Asia, Africa, and Latin America), children commonly sleep with one or both parents or with their siblings for several years. In many homes in the United States and other Western industrialized countries, where independence is highly valued and space less an issue, toddlers are much less likely to sleep with their parents.
- In some Native American tribes, like many other tribal and traditional rural cultures around the world, all members of the family and immediate community are expected to help raise a child, whether or not the child's mother is around. Grandmothers, aunts, male relatives, and older siblings frequently share the responsibilities. This is one of the main reasons that even in the United States, Latin American, Somali, and other immigrant families from traditional cultures are less likely to put their children in preschools or child care.

- In more and more countries today, particularly industrialized and technologically advanced countries such as the United States, Europe, and parts of Asia, mothers from a variety of cultural backgrounds either choose to work or are forced to work out of financial need, and then rely on others outside of the home for child care.
- In some tribal and rural cultures in Africa, Asia, and South America, infants and toddlers are carried all day long while their mothers go about their daily chores. Whether tied on their mothers' backs or carried in a sling or pouch at their mothers' sides, child and mother are rarely separated, and the child may be breast-fed on demand throughout the day. Some children are carried this way until the age of two, three, or even four.
- In contrast, infants and toddlers in Western cultures are generally carried upright, peering over the shoulders of their parents or caregivers, and they are often carried in a variety of devices, such as strollers, carriages, car seats, and other carriers.

LEARNING CULTURAL SENSITIVITY

The way people carry out routine tasks when caring for infants and toddlers is based on the way they were raised in their own families. It may also be influenced by their education and other experiences. Given how culturally diverse the United States is becoming, you may be working with families whose caregiving practices are very different from your own. Sometimes this may cause conflict. You can show cultural sensitivity by listening respectfully to their concerns and involving the family in resolving conflicts. To work together successfully, you must try to understand caregiving practices that are different or unfamiliar and be willing to give them a try.

Cultural sensitivity is actually an attitude. Once you're aware of your own cultural views and attitudes, you can make changes to them. Of course, it's not possible to resolve all cultural differences. Sometimes, differences can only be managed and accepted. What's really important is to talk to parents with an open mind and a respectful attitude. When caregivers and parents come together to share information about caregiving practices, both gain an understanding and an appreciation of each other's family culture, and that understanding can enrich and connect all of us.

Thinking about such cultural issues and questions can help you look at and understand your own beliefs. If you know how much culture affects a child's development and learning, you can appreciate the many different experiences young children have on their way to becoming adults.

Despite the wide differences in child-rearing and education practices among cultures, we still need to answer a basic question for all children: What are the common goals of child growth and development? Today, child development experts distinguish four basic goals for all growing children:

- learning to control their emotions, behaviors, and attention
- developing language and the ability to think and solve problems
- learning to relate to others and to form and keep friendships
- achieving and maintaining healthy bodies and taking on more and more responsibility for their own health and safety

THE STORY OF TWO FAMILIES

You may remember Angela and Jeremy from the first book in this series, Understanding Infant Development. *Jeremy came into the world as a healthy baby under excellent conditions and with mature parents. Angela was not as fortunate, having been born prematurely to a young, inexperienced mother. The story of Jeremy and Angela's development continues in this book.*

In this chapter, we've discussed theories of physical and motor development and how cultural attitudes and practices can affect these aspects of infants' growth. Next, we'll turn our attention to toddlers' physical, motor, and perceptual growth and competence. You'll learn about expected growth patterns and developmental milestones and how important it is for adults to recognize physical and motor problems in young children as early as possible.

2 Physical and Motor Competence

General Physical Characteristics

The rapid growth we see in infancy slows somewhat during the second year. Body proportions begin to change—from the short, rounded characteristics of the one-year-old to the thinner, more muscular look of a three-year-old. Early attempts to walk create a posture typical of toddlers: stomach pushed out, arms held upward, and feet spread wide apart for balance. By age three, changes in toddlers' bodies and proportions give them a look that is leaner and more upright, making walking noticeably easier.

Facial proportions are also changing. The infant and young child have rather high, round, and prominent foreheads, resulting from early and rapid brain and cranial growth. Because of this early growth pattern, facial features make up a smaller portion of the facial area than they do as the child gets older. Over the next few years, facial proportions change and the child will lose the "baby face."

Expected Growth Patterns and Developmental Milestones

By the end of the first year, healthy infants have mastered such motor skills as rolling over, sitting without help, crawling, pulling up, and sometimes even standing alone. Between the ages of ten and fifteen months, infants may start to walk when held by one hand or they may pull themselves up to a standing position and "cruise" by holding on to furniture. These activities are called *large-motor* activities because they use and coordinate the large muscles of the arms, trunk, and legs. Because these muscles generally mature earliest, children master large-muscle skills sooner than small-muscle skills, such as handling a spoon, a crayon, or buttons.

LARGE-MOTOR DEVELOPMENT

Large-motor development follows predictable patterns. When you look at table 2.1, which identifies *developmental milestones* for ages one to four, you'll notice the impressive number of large-motor skills that appear during the first thirty-six months. This table is based on the average development parents and child care professionals can expect to see. Of course, for all types of growth, there are individual differences in the rate and order of development. Being aware of the expected order in which these traits appear will help you know what to expect—and when to be concerned if a child in your care is falling significantly behind other children of similar age.

Table 2.1: Developmental Milestones in Large-Motor Development from Ages One to Four

Age	Motor Development
12 to 18 months	Pulls self up to standing position holding on to furniture
	Throws objects from crib
	Walks when both hands are held
	Crawls up steps
	Rolls a large ball using both hands and arms
	Attempts to slide from lap or high chair
	Begins to make the change from crawling to walking
	Stands alone
	Climbs onto a chair
	Takes two or three steps without support with legs widespread and arms held forward for balance
	Gets into a standing position without help
	Squats to pick up an object
	Reverts to crawling when in a hurry rather than attempting to walk
	Cannot yet make sudden stops or turns
	"Dances" in place to music

18 to 24 months	Bends to pick up objects
	Walks without falling
	Pulls or drags toys
	Seats self in a child's chair
	Walks up and down stairs assisted
	Walks backward
	"Dances" to music, moving about
	Mimics household activities: bathing baby, sweeping, dusting, talking on telephone
24 to 36 months	Runs
	Walks on toes
	Jumps in place
	Kicks a large ball
	Imitates rhythms and animal movements; for example, gallops like a horse, waddles like a duck
	Throws a ball
	Catches a rolling ball
	Jumps in place
	Rides a tricycle
	Walks stairs one step at a time
	Jumps from lowest step
	Attempts to balance standing on one foot
36 to 48 months	Balances on one foot
	Hops, gallops, runs with ease
	Avoids obstacles
	Stops readily
	Walks on a line
	Jumps over low objects
	Throws a ball, directed
	Enjoys simple dances and rhythms

SMALL-MOTOR DEVELOPMENT

Small-motor development is equally dramatic, but not always as obvious as large-muscle growth. The ability to reach, hold, manipulate, and let go of objects improves rapidly during the second year, as does coordination between hands and eyes. With their increasing ability to move around, known as *locomotor ability*, and their improving hand–eye coordination, toddlers turn their attention in earnest to exploring the world around them. Successful exploration depends on the refinement of large muscles, small muscles, vision, and hearing.

Definition: *Locomotor ability*—movement or the power to move from one place to another.

By age one, young children generally have the ability to use their thumbs and fingers to hold an object. Activities such as pouring objects from a container and then putting them back into it, one by one—which requires both grasping and releasing—can hold a toddler's attention for some time.

Table 2.2 shows expected patterns and developmental milestones for small-motor development from ages one through four. Remember, though, that many biological and environmental influences affect both the order and timing of motor skill development. In addition, cultural expectations, food quality, general health and well-being, and opportunities and encouragement to use these new abilities can also influence development.

Table 2.2: Developmental Milestones in Small-Motor Development from Ages One to Four

Age	Motor Development
12 to 18 months	Picks up small objects with a pinching movement
	Drops and picks up toys
	Drops a toy into a container
	Knocks over a tower with a wave of the hand
	Throws things to the floor
	Feeds self easily with fingers
	Uses a spoon clumsily
	Stacks two cubes after seeing it done
	Pours objects from a container
	Builds a tower of three or four cubes
	Holds two cubes in one hand
	Takes off shoes, socks
	Points to things
	Uses a cup for drinking
	Feeds self efficiently
18 to 24 months	Uses a spoon and a cup clumsily
	Turns pages of a book, two and three pages at a time
	Places large pegs in a peg board
	Holds a crayon with a fist
	Writes or draws meaningless marks
	Squeezes a soft squeak-toy
24 to 36 months	Builds a tower of five to seven cubes
	Strings three or four large beads together
	Turns the pages of a book one at a time
	Tries to draw lines and circles
	Manages a spoon and a cup with increasing efficiency
	Lines up objects in a row

36 to 48 months	Builds a tower of eight to ten cubes
	Draws various shapes
	Feeds self with few spills
	Unbuttons front of clothing
	Handles various simple fasteners, including zippers
	Works puzzles of three to six pieces
	Handles books efficiently
	Exhibits hand preference
	Spreads butter and jam on toast
	Dresses and undresses with assistance

Vision and Hearing

Growth and development are greatly affected by the health and normal functioning of toddlers' senses, especially vision and hearing. While a normal adult's *visual acuity* (how well one sees) is 20/20, a newborn's is about 20/600. This means that the newborn sees an object that is 20 feet away with the same clarity as an adult would at 600 feet away. Infants' vision improves quickly over the first six months to about 20/100, and by age three, children's visual quality usually reaches about 20/30. It's not until around age five that children reach what is considered normal vision of 20/20.

Because children's vision changes and develops so quickly during the first years, doctors recommend that they have regular eye examinations to detect any problems as early as possible. Children who received oxygen at birth, were premature, had a low birth weight, or have birth defects are at high risk for eye problems.

As a child care professional, you will be in a position to see behaviors and physical characteristics that might indicate vision problems. The symptoms in infants and toddlers are listed on the next page. If you see any of these symptoms, it's important to tell the child's parents and suggest a professional evaluation by a pediatrician.

Growth and development are greatly affected by the health and normal functioning of toddlers' senses, especially vision and hearing.

BEHAVIORS SUGGESTIVE OF VISUAL PROBLEMS IN INFANTS AND TODDLERS

- Regular or constant misalignment of one or both eyes, such as crossing of the eyes
- Eyeballs that flutter quickly from side to side or up and down
- Inability to follow a moving object
- A white pupil, which may indicate a cataract or other problem
- Pain or redness in one or both eyes
- Constant watery eyes
- Sensitivity to light
- Thick, colored fluid from the eye
- Frequent squinting or rubbing the eyes
- Unusual tilting or turning the head "to see"
- Eyelids that droop
- Eyes that appear to bulge

Hearing, like vision, greatly affects the growth and development of young children, and as with vision, early diagnosis and treatment of problems are very important. Hearing problems interfere with children's ability to understand speech and if unnoticed or untreated, can delay speech and language development, and can eventually result in permanent hearing loss.

It's difficult to notice hearing loss in infants by just watching them. Without a test at the time of birth, hearing loss may not be noticed before a child is one or two years old—an age at which important opportunities for help and treatment have been missed. The more severe the hearing problem, the more likely that it will be noticed by parents or child care professionals. Children with hearing problems may show any one or a combination of the behaviors listed below. When children are old enough to indicate that they do or do not hear a sound, they should be examined by a hearing specialist.

BEHAVIORS SUGGESTIVE OF HEARING PROBLEMS IN INFANTS AND TODDLERS

- Failing to turn in the direction of sounds
- Pulling or rubbing ears
- Staring at a speaker's mouth
- Being easily surprised by sounds

- Being inattentive
- Failing to follow directions
- Having delayed speech and language development
- Having frequent earaches, colds, or allergies

Perceptual-Motor Development

Perception is the process of using our senses to take in information about the world around us. It involves all of our senses. For instance, seeing, or visual perception, gives us the ability to recognize and see the differences in faces, patterns, sizes, shapes, depth, distance, and so on. Hearing, or auditory perception, also gives us information to identify people, objects, and events, and together with sight, helps us make sense of such qualities as distance, speed, and space. Our ability to feel things gives us important information about textures, temperature, weight, and pressure, as well as our own body position and movements. Our ability to smell and taste provide additional information—and pleasure too.

Perceptual-motor development refers to the relationships between a child's perceptions and his motor responses. Motor abilities can influence perceptual development, and perception can have a strong effect on motor skill development. Toddlers' locomotor experiences help them develop a sense of space, depth, and weight. When a child sees a large, hollow block, she might first think it will be very heavy, only lift it and discover that the block is really quite light. Such motor experiences are necessary for children to develop a perception of weight.

Toddlers who have little chance to play with other children or toys, who are kept in playpens, or who spend hours in front of televisions every day will likely have delayed perceptual-motor development.

Likewise, their motor development depends on the normal functioning of their vision and hearing. For a child to successfully reach for a ball and pick it up, he must integrate visual information about where the ball is in relation to his arm.

Toddlers need many experiences like these, ones that involve all their senses, to develop and integrate their perceptual and motor abilities. They need a safe environment where they can use their senses of sight, hearing, and touch to plan and carry out motor activities. Playing with toys, climbing on objects, running, rolling around, building things with blocks or Legos—all the activities that children naturally do—are ways that they unconsciously develop their perceptual-motor skills. Imitating another child's scribbles is an example of visual-motor integration. Responding to the rhythms of music is an example of audio-motor integration. Curling into one's own cubby at a child care center is an example of *kinesthetic-*

motor integration. Thus, if infants and toddlers have little chance to play with other children or toys, are kept in playpens, or spend hours in front of televisions every day, they will likely have delayed perceptual-motor development.

> Definition: *Kinesthesis*—being aware of one's body, its position, and its movement.

At thirteen months, Jeremy is aware of his parents' delight as they watch him take his first steps. Feet spread wide, arms bent at the elbows, reaching upward for balance, he lifts one foot to step, loses his balance, and tumbles sideways. On the next attempt, he is able to toddle two or three steps before falling. His new skill is thrilling but also somewhat frightening. His parents clap, laugh, coax, and praise him with every attempt. Soon, however, he gets tired from the effort and the excitement, and he goes back to a more familiar and efficient way of moving around. Back down on his hands and knees, he quickly and easily crawls to his father's open arms.

Jeremy's parents have tried to provide space for Jeremy's increasing ability to move around the house. They arranged the furniture so that it's out of his way, covered sharp edges, and removed things he could trip on.

Now that he is learning to walk, his mother helps him with his stair-climbing skills. Holding both hands from behind him, Ann walks Jeremy to the three steps. At first, Jeremy puts one foot forward into the air and then brings it back to the level of the first step, as though he were walking on a level surface. As a result, his mother has to "save" him from falling down the steps. Not too happy with all this work, Jeremy again drops into a crawling position, turns, and goes down the steps backward.

Jeremy's motor behaviors illustrate some important aspects of perceptual-motor development. Limited perception of space and speed prompted his parents to arrange their living spaces to accommodate his poorly coordinated movements. His lack of depth perception is shown by Ann's experiment. His visual, kinesthetic, and depth perception have not yet become coordinated. At thirteen months, Jeremy simply needs more time to integrate his visual-motor abilities. It will be some time before he's able to go down steps in an upright-forward position. (Typically, children do not descend stairs smoothly and without help until around age four.)

Visual-motor development grows through opportunities to practice locomotor and small-motor skills. Body awareness, balance, rhythm, space, and temporal awareness increase as toddlers explore their surroundings and experience their body movements and abilities.

> *Toddlers need an environment where they can experiment with the world around them—a place where they can use their senses to play with toys, climb, run, roll around, and build with blocks or Legos. This is how they unconsciously develop their perceptual-motor skills.*

At thirteen months, Angela's motor development is somewhat delayed. As a premature baby, her motor skills are about four to six months behind children her age who were full-term. In spite of this delay, her development appears quite normal, though she is often more excitable, more restless, and more easily frustrated than other children her age—not unusual for premature infants. She is always very excited to explore the house when outside of her playpen or crib.

Cheryl has had a happy and successful year at her new school. With help from her school's child care center, Cheryl is learning to balance parenting and school. She is taking a child development course and is very interested in learning about the different stages Angela is going through and the new abilities she is developing. Cheryl is just learning to provide a home environment where Angela can safely explore. As yet, Angela is often put in the playpen, sometimes for a long time. She cruises around the playpen, watches the other children, listens to the television, and cuddles with her soft toys. She enjoys dropping small blocks into a bucket and then dumping them out. The older children bring her other things to play with, and when she gets fussy, they talk with her and play games like peek-a-boo or "Which hand is the toy in?" Angela's environment is verbally rich and interactive, though often it can be overstimulating.

With little chance to explore her world, Angela's perceptual-motor integration has been even further delayed. Limited opportunities to develop these skills could put Angela at risk for learning difficulties later on.

Toddlers with Special Needs

Children with special needs often experience health and developmental problems. These can include chronic illnesses, disabilities and developmental delays, malnutrition, and psychological troubles. It's very important for adults who care for at-risk toddlers to recognize any physical or motor problems as early as possible, to guide their primary caregivers to treatment programs, and to provide support in the following areas:

1. General health and nutritional needs
2. Ongoing assessment of physical and motor abilities, with special attention to locomotor and large- and small-motor skills, including:
   a. posture
   b. reflexes
   c. balance
   d. flexibility
   e. voluntary movements
   f. "transitional" movements (moving from sitting to standing, for example)
   g. hand-eye, eye-foot, and hand-mouth coordination
   h. holding and releasing abilities
   i. chewing and swallowing abilities
   j. mobility preference patterns
3. Muscle problems and physical deformities that can develop after long use of abnormal movement patterns (Sexton 1990)

If disabling conditions are recognized early in a child's development, they often can be treated and improved. Paying attention to the growth and development of the children you care for will help you see any unusual developmental problems and respond to them in an appropriate way.

Many types of intervention programs and services are available for children and families with special needs in intervention programs for toddlers with special needs. Parents and child care professionals can take a number of the steps involved:

- meeting the child's immediate physical, health, and psychological requirements
- helping parents adjust their parenting skills to meet the needs of their special child
- providing instruction and support systems for parents
- adapting home and out-of-home child care arrangements
- providing ongoing assessments and therapies as needed
- providing assistive technologies as needed to improve self-help efforts

- providing activities and daily routines that will help the child's physical and motor development
- coordinating services needed by the child and the family
- providing high-quality early childhood education programs and skilled professionals to ensure the best possible developmental progress

Reference

Sexton, D. 1990. Quality integrated programs for infants and toddlers with special needs. In *Personalizing care with infants, toddlers and families.* Ed. E. Stubeck and M. F. Kelley. Olney, Md: Association for Childhood Education International.

3 The Relationship between Physical/Motor and Psychosocial Development

Physical/motor development and psychosocial development are strongly tied to one another. Each new motor skill helps build a toddler's sense of self-worth. Toddlers' increasing sense of their own abilities, as well as their relationships with parents, caregivers, and other adults in their lives, builds a foundation for the development of *self-concept*.

> Definition: *Self-concept*—the whole inner picture that we have of ourselves, including our beliefs about how competent we are, our value as a person, whether we deserve to be loved and cared for, and our attractiveness.

Toddlers and some older infants reveal their emerging self-concept when they focus on certain aspects of their bodies and their new abilities. These include:

Physical/motor development and psychosocial development are strongly tied to one another. Each new motor skill helps build a toddler's sense of self-worth.

- pointing to and naming their body parts
- telling you their names, holding up the correct number of fingers to show their ages, and saying, "Look at me!" as they show a new skill
- insisting on doing things for themselves such as taking off their socks and shoes, holding their spoons or cups, and preferring to walk rather than be carried

These and similar actions show toddlers' emerging body awareness and self-awareness. Their increasing efforts to be self-sufficient, their growing awareness of gender differences, and their growing control of their bladder and bowels are further indications of self-concept development.

Self-Help Efforts

Children's growing desire to do things for themselves emerges early when infants want to hold their bottles, use their hands and fingers to feed themselves, take and let go of toys and other belongings, and effectively communicate their needs to others with their voices, words, or body language. Toddlers' emerging sense of self contributes to their increasing desire for independence.

A toddler's increasing motor skills and ability to move around by himself improves his growing self-help skills. Awkward yet determined attempts at dressing and undressing, feeding himself, using a washcloth to wash his face after meals, and washing his hands after toileting are examples of early self-help abilities.

Of course, spills, accidents, and delays are common at this time. Parents and child care professionals must be patient, supportive, and encouraging during these often boring, time-consuming, and sometimes frustrating early efforts. As toddlers become more successful in their attempts to do things on their own, their sense of pride and self-worth grows. As a result, they are even more motivated to continue their efforts. And with practice, they become more and more efficient.

As we will discuss in the next chapter, it is important that parents and caregivers support children's early attempts at independence in order for healthy psychosocial development to proceed. When parents or other caregivers respond to these early self-help efforts by yelling, punishing, or making other negative responses, they discourage young children. Such responses can lead to dependent, defiant, and other negative behaviors.

If parents and caregivers recognize that these efforts are an important part of a toddler's growth and development, they can anticipate how long it takes for a child to complete these tasks and give her the time she needs. If time is a problem, decide how much the child can do while you, the caregiver, do other tasks. You could say, for example, "I'll pack the bag while you put on your socks, then I'll put on one shoe and you put on the other. You get your blanket while I get your sweater, then you will be ready to go when your dad comes to pick you up." Being patient and giving young children extra time to complete these tasks helps them develop confidence in their abilities to do things for themselves.

Body and Gender Awareness

Toddlers' awareness of their bodies grows with each new motor skill they develop. Throwing an object from the crib, pulling themselves up to a standing position and dropping back to a seated one, dumping toys from a container, climbing a staircase, and opening a drawer are just some of the many activities that toddlers like to do. Once they discover a new motor ability, they will repeat it several times. Simply repeating a new skill is great fun for them. Toddlers have a built-in desire to grow and develop that drives them to perform actions over and over again until a new challenge grabs their attention. Encouragement and praise from their caregivers gives them even more motivation to explore and grow. Mastering skills gives them a sense of control and power, along with an increased awareness of their capabilities. For toddlers and their caregivers, this is a thrilling time, but it's also a time when careful supervision is critical.

A toddler's increasing ability to name body parts also supports body awareness. Toddlers enjoy learning the names of their body parts: eyes, ears, nose, mouth, feet, toes, stomach, ribs, and so on. Naming body parts can often become a game: the adult asks the toddler the names of different parts of his body and shows excitement at the toddler's answers. These early body awareness experiences are signs that toddlers are beginning to develop a sense of identity that includes gender and gender-related behaviors.

Gender awareness, becoming aware that there is a difference between males and females, begins during the first year and is usually established by age two-and-a-half to three. *Gender identity* involves labeling oneself and others according to gender, an assessment that is usually based on external features such as the clothing people wear, the toys they own or play with, the way they wear their hair, and so on. Very young children often assume that simply by changing these outside features, they can become the opposite gender.

Definition: *Gender awareness*—the understanding that men and women, girls and boys, are different.

Definition: *Gender identity*—the awareness of being either male or female.

Toddlers also show their new gender awareness with curiosity about their own and others' bodies. Curiosity about the body parts of others is generally open and straightforward. Toddlers may touch their mothers' breasts, watch intently as their dads urinate, become curious about the body parts of a brother or sister, and explore their own genitalia. These behaviors are simply signs of normal curiosity. They are harmless and indicate the child's growing body awareness and the early stages of sexuality. Just as other kinds of human functioning do, sexuality develops in stages from infancy through adulthood.

Childhood Sexuality

Childhood sexuality and adult sexuality are very different. Childhood sexuality involves curiosity and play, spontaneity and openness, sensuality and excitement. To this, adult sexuality adds privacy, passion, eroticism, and self-consciousness. Adults are aware of their sexuality (and the consequences of their sexual behavior).

The meanings that young children attach to gender differences and sexual behaviors are very different from those of adults. Children's sexuality is characterized by a simple interest in the body and its functions, labels for body parts, and experiments with adult language related to the body and its functions. Young children are usually quite comfortable with their bodies and are not usually concerned about privacy—a behavior we learn. For these reasons, toddlers are open and direct with their questions and curiosity. These behaviors often worry or disturb American adults, particularly if the adults attach adult meanings and their own feelings and values to the behaviors, failing to recognize that young children's behaviors are not accompanied by the sexual desires that happen in adolescent and adult sexuality.

Basically, toddlers are just curious. They have many questions about why girls and boys are different, why they use the toilet in different ways, how babies "get in a mommy's tummy," why girls don't have penises and the like. To them, the world is full of surprises and mysteries, and wanting to know why girls don't have penises isn't any different than wondering why a red rubber ball bounces and a red wooden ball doesn't.

Toddlers' questions about gender and sexuality should be answered in simple, sensitive, and nonjudgmental ways. Answer them as they arise, without deferring to another adult or putting it off until a later time. Matter-of-fact answers are all they need at this age. Oftentimes, just naming the body parts is sufficient.

What is most important is that children feel comfortable asking questions about human anatomy, gender, and sexuality. Surprise, embarrassment, or scolding can get in the way of healthy communication and convey negative messages about the human body—both the child's body and the bodies of others.

It's also important to avoid discussions that are either too technical or too value laden. You needn't explain how every body part works. However, it is important to use correct terms, such as *urinate*, *bowel movement*, *breasts*, and *penis*, because doing so helps prevent confusion as children grow older. Talk about and set clear limits about public versus personal behaviors, modesty and privacy, and appropriate language.

Toilet Learning

In infancy, the elimination of body wastes simply happens—it's an unconscious reflex. Learning to use a toilet takes place gradually, over a period of years, as infants' bodies mature. It is not, as the term *toilet training* suggests, something that can be taught at a certain age. Instead, parents *and* caregivers need to learn to respond to a child's signals that he has begun to pay attention to this process. Because so many infants and toddlers now spend at least some time in child care centers, the majority of toilet learning happens there, not in their homes. As a result, it's quite important that child care professionals understand this process too.

Toilet learning actually depends on complex neurological development. During the first year or so, infants must develop a conscious awareness of bowel and bladder fullness and the muscles controlling elimination. (Usually bowel control happens before bladder control.) But this control can't happen until certain nerve pathways have developed and matured. In addition, infants must have some language and locomotor skills to signal their need to caregivers. They must have the motor skills needed to get to a toilet in time, to remove clothing, and then to actually use the toilet. These are not easy tasks for toddlers! These abilities all develop over an extended time. Using a toilet is a relatively challenging activity well into the preschool years.

Because so many infants and toddlers now spend at least some time in child care centers, the majority of toilet learning happens there, not in their homes.

THE FIRST SIGNS OF READINESS

Between the ages of eighteen and twenty months, toddlers begin to signal that they're aware of dirty diapers. They may, for example, try to remove the diaper or use words or motions to describe their need to urinate or defecate. Getting too excited about these signs and expecting that a child will soon have control may lead to disappointment. Attempts to set a toileting schedule will probably fail. On the other hand, if caregivers are aware of the times of day when toileting seems to occur regularly—for example, first thing in the morning, soon after breakfast, or on waking from a nap—they can gently ask or remind the child, helping her notice the need to go to the toilet.

Pushing children to use the toilet, or scolding, shaming, or punishing them, will only cause more problems. It will slow the process by creating stress, anxiety, or power control situations that have negative effects on the child, adult, and their relationship. Toddlers' caregivers need to be patient, helpful, and encouraging as toilet learning proceeds. Toileting accidents, which will happen frequently before toddlers master this complicated task, should be treated respectfully.

Some children may achieve control over toileting by age two, others may lack such control until age three or four, and still others may not be free of occasional accidents before age five or six. Even after control seems

> *Pushing children to use the toilet, or scolding, shaming, or punishing them, will only cause more problems and slow the process by creating stress, anxiety, or power control situations.*

to be established, children will have accidents for a variety of reasons: illness, diarrhea, bladder infection, sound sleep, distraction (too busy to notice the need), excitement, anxiety, or upsetting experiences are all good reasons. Toddlers sometimes fall back to the precontrol stage when family life changes in some way: a move to a new house, the birth of a new baby, the hospitalization of a family member, a death or divorce in the family. It can happen even due to an unusually exciting or happy event, such as a birthday party or holiday celebration.

Parents and child care professionals should *expect* uneven development in toilet learning and should not show disappointment when the toddler is unsuccessful. When the adults in the toddler's life are supportive during this stage, they help ensure continued success as well as healthy attitudes toward the human body and elimination.

In chapter 4, we will look at the complicated relationship between physical/motor and cognitive development. We'll see how children's environments, and their ability to explore them, can have a strong influence on early neurological development.

4 The Relationship between Physical/Motor and Cognitive Development

The human brain is made up of billions of nerve cells, or neurons, which begin developing while the child is still in the mother's womb. Unlike other cells in the body, however, neurons are not packed closely together—they have spaces between them that allow them to connect or communicate with one another. During infancy and the toddler period, growth of these nerve cells and the connections between them, called *synapses*, increases rapidly.

As neurons develop, their growth and survival depend on environmental stimulation, which triggers new synapses. The quality and quantity of early stimulation can have long-term effects on cognitive development. Neurons not stimulated tend to die. On the other hand, neurons exposed to environments that are rich in sensory stimulation—sights, sounds, smells, tastes, and touching and moving—grow and develop.

Increased Motor Abilities Affect Cognitive Development

Early brain growth first influences motor abilities, and then sensory perceptions. Similarly, children's earliest motor abilities can have a great influence on their cognitive development. Toddlers' increasing ability to get around—walking, running, climbing, reaching—and amazing curiosity lead them into an ever-expanding world of exploration, experimentation, and discovery. The role of parents and child care workers is to provide spaces and opportunities for the toddler to explore, rich sensory experiences, engaging conversations about objects and events surrounding the child, and satisfying social interactions. The richer the toddlers' experiences, the more promising the effects on their neurological development, brain growth, and cognitive performance. (More information about physical, motor, and cognitive development can be found in the first book of this series, *Understanding Infant Development*, chapters 6 and 10.)

Unfortunately, the opposite is also true. Being deprived, neglected, or abused during these formative times can have long-lasting negative brain effects. Neuroscientists now know that stressful or traumatic experiences in infancy and early childhood—if they continue for a long time—can actually affect neurological development and harm brain function. Additionally, toddlers who are deprived of an environment rich in sensory experiences, or who have inconsistent care from adults, may show cognitive delays.

> *The richer the toddlers' experiences, the more promising the effects on their neurological development, brain growth, and cognitive performance.*

Experts in child development now believe that a strong, secure attachment to a nurturing caregiver actually can provide biological protection for infants against the later effects of stress or trauma. Furthermore, school-age children who have had secure attachment relationships during infancy and early childhood develop fewer behavior problems when they encounter stressful or traumatic experiences.

EXPERIMENTS SUPPORT THE NEED FOR RICH ENVIRONMENTS

In the first three years, windows of opportunity—sensitive periods in brain growth—open for the following:

- developing social attachment (birth to two years)
- learning to control or change emotions (birth to two years)
- developing the ability to cope with stress (birth to three years)

Much of what we know about windows of opportunity was learned in animal studies. One of the first studies took place in the 1960s by a group of researchers at the University of California at Berkeley (Diamond, Krech, and Rosenzweig 1964). They examined the brain size and thickness of rats that had been raised in two kinds of cages: an "enriched" cage, where they lived with other rats and had "toys" to play with, and a small cage without playmates or toys.

The experiments clearly showed that the rats raised in the "enriched" cage were much better at finding their way through mazes than the rats raised in the "boring" cage. Furthermore, the "enriched" rats actually had a thicker *cerebral cortex* than the other rats. Thus, differences in early life experiences can affect the actual structure of the brain.

Definition: *Cerebral cortex*—the outer layer of the front part of the brain, which is primarily responsible for higher-level nerve functions. In humans, it is the part of the brain where reasoning takes place and the site of self-awareness.

What do these and similar studies tell us about the human brain? We now know that enriched and mentally stimulating environments increase the growth of neurons and synapses in humans too—and they also thicken the human cerebral cortex. Further, scientists can trace various types of development—vision, hearing, motor controls, language, and so on—through periods of sensitive and rapid growth when certain experiences have a greater effect, that is, during windows of opportunity. While brain enrichment is possible throughout our lives, childhood and adolescence appear to be the best period for brain development—a time when neural growth and connections are most productive.

Children in the toddler stage are still experiencing rapid growth in many areas, and a number of factors influence their physical, neurological, and motor development. In chapter 5, you'll learn about some of them, including more about toddlers' nutritional needs and about how you, as a child care professional, can help their development by providing toys and materials that promote motor development and that support their need to explore, play, and interact. Because toddlers are both curious and inexperienced, we'll also learn important steps you must take to lessen their risk of accidents and injury. Finally, we'll take note of the appropriate expectations for toddler-age children.

Reference
Diamond, M. C., D. Krech, and M. R. Rosenzweig. 1964. "The effects of an enriched environment on the histology of the rat cerebral cortex." *Journal of Comparative Neurology* 123:111–119.

5 Factors Influencing Physical and Motor Development

Many diverse factors can affect the rate, order, and quality of toddlers' physical and motor development. Caregivers can affect some of them in the form of a healthy diet, proper rest, the timely prevention and treatment of illnesses, and provisions for a safe and intellectually stimulating environment.

Nutrition

Good nutrition provides the nutrients young children need to grow and develop strong minds and bodies; it provides the energy required to play, think, and learn. On the other hand, poor nutrition can cause delayed neurological and physical development, slower cognitive functioning, weaker immune systems, increased incidence of diseases, and vulnerability to toxins in the environment. During these early years of growth and development, it is particularly important to ensure that a child receives proper nutrition.

You can help toddlers learn to eat and enjoy the types of food that ensure proper nutrition by:

- offering a wide selection of nutritious foods
- preparing and presenting new foods in an appealing way
- creating a social and emotional environment at mealtimes that helps toddlers enjoy their food and the ritual of eating
- respecting toddlers' food preferences and the amount of food they feel comfortable eating

CHOOSE HEALTHY FOODS

A toddler's daily dietary plan should include food from the following groups:

- breads, cereals, rice, and pasta
- vegetables and fruits
- milk, yogurt, and cheese
- meat, poultry, fish, beans, and eggs
- fats, oils, and sweets (very few)

Fatty foods and sweets don't have to be eliminated from toddlers' diets, but they should be included with care. High-fructose corn syrup is a particular problem because it contains far more calories than cane sugar while having no nutritional value whatsoever.

Toddlers are just beginning to try many solid foods and drinks other than milk. This means that they are discovering a variety of tastes, textures, and colors. How easily toddlers accept new foods depends on how they look and smell, what they feel like in their mouths, and, of course, how they taste. Encouraging children to taste new foods, but not insisting that they eat a whole serving, gives them a chance to learn about the food in a positive way. It respects the fact that there are foods they may never like—just as we adults have foods we simply don't like.

Toddlers are gaining independence in feeding themselves. Finger feeding, using a spoon, and drinking from a cup all support their growing ability to chew and swallow, as well as their hand-eye and hand-mouth coordination. At their age, it takes focus and concentration to do these things well.

Avoid foods that can cause choking, such as hot dogs; meat (beef, pork, chicken) in chunks that are too large and too tough to chew and swallow easily; peanuts and other nuts; popcorn; grapes; carrots; round hard candies; stiff chewy candies (taffy, caramels); and chewing gum.

Toddlers' appetites change from meal to meal and day to day. Tastes and food preferences also vary from day to day, often for little or no reason. Healthy children generally eat enough food to satisfy themselves. Especially when growing, children often are hungry between meals, so healthy snacks should be available for them. Avoiding unhealthy sugary or fatty snacks between meals will make it more likely that the child will take in essential nutrients in the regular meals that are provided.

Sleep Patterns

Getting enough sleep and rest contributes to the general health and well-being of the toddler. Children need less sleep as they get older. Toddlers may take one or two short naps or one long nap during the day and sleep anywhere from eight to twelve hours at night.

Toddlers are social beings and they may resist bedtime. These years are marked by a growing sense of independence, but also by a fear of separation. These issues may complicate bedtime and naptime rituals. Regular and predictable routines help toddlers accept the separation and get to sleep more easily. Here is a familiar sequence: bath, bedtime story, brushing teeth, saying good night to family members, spending a few moments of quiet with a parent, and, finally, turning the lights off and the nightlight on.

General Health and Freedom from Disease

Because infectious diseases can spread quickly among children in groups, child care and early education programs often have attendance and participation policies. The National Resource Center for Health and Safety in Child Care, the American Public Health Association, and the American Academy of Pediatrics (2002) published recommended guidelines and policies for early childhood programs in *Caring for Our Children: National Health and Safety Performance Standards: Guidelines for Out-of-Home Child Care Programs*. You can find this and other health and safety topics relating to children in groups by visiting the Web site of the National Resource Center for Health and Safety in Child Care and Early Education at http://nrc.uchsc.edu/CFOC/index.html.

Some obvious signs of potential illness require immediate attention: fever, unusual tiredness, irritability, crying, difficulty breathing, diarrhea, vomiting, mouth sores, rashes, infestations such as head lice, scabies, or symptoms of any communicable disease. As a caregiver, you will be better prepared to deal with these health issues when you know about common symptoms and behaviors, how to respond to children who are sick or hurt, and how to prevent the spread of illness in your program.

All young children get sick and parents are responsible for telling caregivers about their children's particular health care needs. Child care professionals should closely watch the increasing incidence of childhood asthma and the reappearance of diseases once thought eliminated in the United States.

ASTHMA

Childhood asthma is an increasingly common chronic disease that makes airways (bronchial tubes) sensitive to irritants. It affects nearly 1.3 million U.S. children younger than age five. Child care staff may need to examine classrooms and buildings for possible asthma triggers. *All* staff members should know how to respond to a particular child's asthma episode.

REAPPEARANCE OF COMMUNICABLE DISEASES

The reappearance of diseases thought to be under control (whooping cough, measles, chicken pox, and, in particular, tuberculosis) should be of concern to child care professionals.

Because state laws allow exemptions from immunization for religious or philosophical reasons, nonimmunized children who catch a disease like mumps or measles can spread it to others, both adults and other nonimmunized children. The increase in cases of measles, whooping cough, and polio in recent years in the United States has been linked to the following reasons:

- families who did not immunize their children
- immigrants and vacation travelers who have or who carry diseases from locations around the world where the diseases exist
- infections, such as HIV, that weaken a person's immune system
- the fading of immunity as a person enters adulthood

Tuberculosis (TB) has reemerged in recent years as a serious public health problem. In the United States, 10 to 15 million people are infected with the TB bacteria, and one in ten of them will develop active TB at some time in their lives. Early diagnosis and treatment of TB is necessary to prevent the spread of the disease.

Children most at risk for TB are those who:

- are immigrants
- have had contact with someone who has tuberculosis
- live in cities with populations of 250,000 or more
- are, or have been, homeless
- have been exposed to a person with HIV
- have had contact with someone who has spent time in jail
- live in poor areas

Safety

Toddlers are particularly in danger of having accidents—some say, jokingly, that they are "accident magnets"! Toddlers lack experience and judgment, and so they tend to act without thinking. They are also very curious, and their desire to be independent puts them at risk for accident and injury. Adults can raise that level of risk by overestimating toddlers' abilities to perform tasks or make judgements.

Toddlers are very curious, and their desire to be independent puts them at risk for accident and injury.

Table 5.1 (Pillitteri 1992) shows important steps adults can take during to lessen the risk of accidents and injury during the toddler period.

Table 5.1: Important Accident Prevention Measures That Families Should Observe during the Toddler Period (Pillitteri 1992)

Potential Accident Situations	Prevention Measures for Health Teaching
Motor vehicles	Maintain children in car seat, not just seat belt; do not be distracted from safe driving by a child in a car.
	Do not allow child to play outside unsupervised.
	Supervise toddler too young to be left alone on a tricycle.
	Teach safety with pedaling toys (look before crossing driveways; do not cross streets).
Falls	Keep house windows closed or keep secure screens in place.
	Place gates at top and bottom of stairs. Supervise at playgrounds.
	Do not allow child to walk with sharp object in hand or mouth.
	Raise crib rails and make sure they are locked before walking away from crib.
Aspiration	Examine toys for small parts that could be aspirated; remove those that appear dangerous.
	Do not feed a toddler popcorn, peanuts, etc.; urge children not to eat while running. Do not leave a toddler alone with a balloon.

Drowning	Do not leave a toddler alone in a bathtub or near water (including buckets of cleaning water).
Animal bites	Do not allow a toddler to approach strange dogs.
	Supervise child's play with family pets.
Poisoning	Never present medication as candy.
	Buy medicines with childproof safety caps; put away immediately after use.
	Never take medication in front of a child.
	Place all medications and poisons in locked cabinets or on overhead shelves where child cannot reach.
	Never leave medication in parents' purse or pocket, which child can reach.
	Always store food or substances in their original containers.
	Use nonlead-based paint throughout the house.
	Hang plants or set them on high surfaces beyond a toddler's grasp.
	Post telephone number of nearest poison control center by the telephone.
Burns	Buy flame-retardant clothing.
	Turn handles of pots toward back of stove to prevent toddler from reaching up and pulling them down.
	Use a cool-mist vaporizer or remain in room when vaporizer is operating so that child is not tempted to play with it.
	Keep a screen in front of fireplaces or heaters.
	Monitor toddlers carefully when they are near lit candles.
	Do not leave toddlers unsupervised near hot-water faucets.
	Do not allow toddlers to blow out matches (teach that fire is not fun); keep matches out of reach.
	Keep electric wires and cords out of toddler's reach; cover electrical outlets with safety plugs.

General	Know whereabouts of toddlers at all times. Toddlers can climb onto chairs, stools, etc., that they could not manage before; can turn doorknobs and go places they could not go before.
	Be aware that the frequency of accidents increases when the family is under stress and therefore less attentive to children. Special precautions must be taken at these times.
	Some children are more active, curious, and impulsive and therefore more vulnerable to accidents.

Opportunities to Explore and Play

Play is children's "work." They need as many opportunities as possible to interact with caring, kind adults and friendly playmates; to explore safe, interesting places; and to do what children naturally do so well—play. Play gives children the opportunity to use their new and growing skills. Child care professionals can help this process by giving the children they care for toys and materials that encourage the following:

- *large-motor coordination* (for example, wheeled toys; low crawling and climbing equipment; large balls to roll, kick, throw, and bounce; large blocks and construction-type toys; tricycles, wagons)
- *small-motor coordination* (for example, fill-and-pour toys; connecting blocks and manipulative items; stacking toys; items that snap, button, zip)
- *perceptual-motor development* (for example, graduated stacking toys; puzzles with four to five parts; shape-sorting boxes; color-matching games; sound-identification games; texture-matching games; beanbag-toss games; rhythm-and-dance games; obstacle-course games; follow-the-leader games)
- *imitative behaviors and pretend play* (for example, dolls; trucks, cars, airplanes; household items such as plastic dishes; dress-up clothes and costumes of familiar characters)
- *language and literacy* (for example, books and pictures; shared-book experiences; puppets, dolls; audio- and video-recorded sounds, tunes, songs, poems, stories; conversation; field trips; drawing and writing materials)

Have Appropriate Expectations

Because of toddlers' fast growth and development, adults often overestimate their maturity and capabilities. Such assumptions are both physically and psychologically risky. Being aware of expected patterns of development will help you recognize each child's unique abilities and interests—and then guide them into activities that are appropriate for them.

It's also important to remember that toddlers are impulsive; they are not yet able to consider their actions thoughtfully before acting. Their brains simply have not developed enough. For the same reason, young children are not capable of protecting themselves in dangerous situations.

Examples of inappropriate expectations include:

- using writing tools or scissors
- coloring within the lines
- putting on or taking off complicated clothing before they have the muscle ability to do so
- remembering safety rules

Watching toddlers closely will help you recognize what they can safely do. Then you'll be better able to provide activities and materials that fit their developmental abilities and needs.

Here are a few suggestions to help you form proper expectations for the children you work with and to ensure that the activities you give them fit their abilities:

- Notice where they put their energy and interests.
- Pay attention to the questions they ask.
- Watch how well they do various large- and small-motor tasks.
- Notice how they talk about their needs.
- Pay attention to how well they understand, remember, and follow directions and requests.

Too often, parents expect children to develop faster than is physically possible. Sadly, when parents get too frustrated with a child who fails to act as they want, child abuse can result. When a parent or other caregiver expects too much of any child, healthy growth and development can be slowed and the relationship harmed.

Characteristics of healthy environments for young children are listed on the next page.

Healthy Environments for Young Children

Healthy home and child care environments for young children have the following:

1. Enough space. Toddlers need enough space to try out their new and uncoordinated motor skills. When play areas are clear, falls and collisions with furniture happen less often.
2. A clean space. Toddlers like to put their hands, toys, and anything else possible into their mouths. Take care to protect toddlers from infections and disease.
3. A safe space and play materials. Toddlers are eager to try out their new reaching, holding, and mobility skills to satisfy their curiosity. Their environment must be free from obstacles, poisons, sharp edges, small objects, unstable furniture and play equipment, exposed electrical cords and outlets, and so on.
4. Developmentally appropriate play items and equipment. Simply put, toys that are too simple will be boring, and ones that are too complicated will be frustrating. Developmentally appropriate play items are safer and make play more fun and interesting. They also give toddlers experiences that will help them develop their physical, motor, and perceptual skills.
5. Constant supervision. Toddlers are energy in motion. They are constantly moving, playing, and exploring, and with their growing physical, motor, and perceptual abilities, they can quickly get themselves in trouble. For this reason, they must be watched constantly. Safety concerns are very important at this age.
6. Supervised health care. Health care must be supervised by appropriate medical and dental professionals. Proper diet, immunizations, rest, exercise, and specialized medical attention as needed enhance chances for optimal growth and development.

References

Pillitteri, A. 1992. *Maternal and child health nursing.* Philadelphia: Lippincott Williams and Wilkins. Copyright © 1992 by Lippincott Williams and Wilkins. Reprinted with permission from Lippincott Williams and Wilkins.

The Role of the Early Childhood Professional

1. Create and maintain a safe, clean environment.
2. Provide proper nutrition.
3. Use activities that are developmentally appropriate for the children in your care. Also be sure your expectations of these children are appropriate for their age and abilities.
4. Encourage exploration, discovery, and independence.
5. Provide supportive and protective guidance.
6. Encourage positive awareness of body and gender.
7. Provide a variety of materials that encourage both large- and small-motor development.
8. Provide toys and experiences that help perceptual-motor development.
9. Look for signs and symptoms of special needs or illness in the children in your care.
10. Be an example of good health and hygiene behaviors.

Discussion Questions

1. What aspects of your child care practice do you feel are influenced by your sociocultural background? Do the children in your care share your background or do they share each other's background? What modifications might you make in your caregiving practices to be more inclusive of different backgrounds?
2. Based on what you've now read about toddler development, if one toddler is developmentally lagging behind another, should you push him to catch up or allow him to develop at his own pace? At what point should you be concerned that a child in your care is falling so far behind others his age that assessment by a trained professional is warranted?
3. What modifications can you or have you made to your physical setting to encourage toddlers' exploration and large-motor development? What activities can you add or have you added to your curriculum to foster toddlers' small-motor development? Talk with other caregivers in your area to share ideas about materials or tools that can be used to encourage such skill building in toddlers.
4. Are you able to accommodate children with special needs in your program? If not, are there small modifications you could make or some extra training you could participate in that would allow you to accept such children into your program? Check with your licensor or your local resource and referral agency to learn where such training is available.

Further Reading

2002. *Caring for our children: National health and safety performance standards: Guidelines for out-of-home child care programs*. 2nd ed. Washington, D.C. and Elk Grove Village, IL: American Public Health Association and American Academy of Pediatrics.

Chrisman, K., and D. Couchenour. 2002. *Healthy sexuality development: A guide for early childhood educators and families*. Washington, D.C.: National Association for the Education of Young Children.

National Safety Council. 1998. *First aid and CPR: Infants and children*. 3rd ed. Boston: Jones and Bartlett Publishers.

Schiff, D., and S. P. Shelov, eds. 1999. *American Academy of Pediatrics official complete home reference: Guide to your child's symptoms*. New York: Random House.

Wolraich, M. I., ed. 2003. *American Academy of Pediatrics guide to toilet training*. New York: Bantam.

Part Two

Psychosocial Development

Our words should be like a magic canvas upon which a child cannot help but paint a positive picture of himself.

—Haim G. Ginott

It is also clear that one of the best ways to enrich an infant or toddler is through unstinting amounts of affection, to build security and self-esteem that will influence all the child's other experiences, and all further enrichments, throughout life.

—Marian Diamond and Janet Hopson

The toddler period of growth and development means new challenges for parents and caregivers. In their first year, infants are compliant and dependent on their caregivers. Now much will begin to change. The toddler years mark children's first real attempts to become more independent. With bigger, stronger, and more coordinated bodies, together with new cognitive abilities, they are on a mission to explore, interact with, and learn about what is to them a huge, new, and exciting world. New communication skills are emerging, which can lead to new and unexpected behaviors. These new behaviors can at once thrill, confuse, frustrate, and intrigue parents and caregivers.

Since parents and other caregivers must set limits on what toddlers are allowed to do in order to protect them from harm, this time can be frustrating for toddlers as well. They are all too eager to explore the world around them.

In part 2, you'll see that a primary challenge for caregivers is supporting toddlers' opposing needs for dependence and independence. You'll become familiar with current theories and studies on psychosocial development during the toddler years. You'll be able to recognize and understand the importance of social and emotional milestones during this period, and you'll explore factors that influence toddlers' development. You'll also see how adults play a very important role in toddlers' healthy psychosocial development.

Chapter 6 begins with an exploration of toddlers' drive for independence—an important stage, but frustrating for both toddler and caregiver. Attachment behaviors begin to change as toddlers form relationships with children their own age. The significance of temperament, play patterns, and a maturing awareness of self and others is discussed, and the important connection between neurological growth and toddlers' new ability to control frustration is explored.

6 Theories of Psychosocial Development

Psychosocial Theory: Autonomy versus Shame and Doubt

As toddlers begin to trust their environments, the people who care for them, and themselves, they become more independent and self-sufficient. Their efforts to buckle a seat belt, turn a light switch on or off, open a door, and take off socks, shoes, or other clothing are very important to the individual child. If an impatient adult interferes, the result is easily tears and tantrums. Where toddlers once welcomed help, they now prefer to do tasks on their own. As toddlers gain confidence in walking, climbing, running, moving, and manipulating objects, locomotion skills and new fine-motor control encourage this independence. You can see their new drive for independence in what they say: "Me do it!" "No!" and "Mine!" While these behaviors strain adult patience, they represent healthy psychosocial development.

According to Erik Erikson's theory of psychosocial development, the toddler is entering a period in which the psychological "conflict" to be resolved is that of autonomy versus shame and doubt. *Autonomy* means independence, and this stage of development lasts from about fifteen months to three years.

Definition: *Autonomy*—a sense of independence or self-regulation.

From birth to about eighteen months, developing a sense of trust (versus mistrust) is a critical psychosocial task. Gaining a healthy sense of trust—which comes through consistent and predictable care—is perhaps the most important achievement in a young child's psychosocial development. Its healthy development creates the foundation for successful completion of the next stage.

When infants can trust their parents and other caregivers, their sense of autonomy will develop more easily and strongly. Erikson believed that the psychosocial opposite of autonomy is shame or doubt. Adults help toddlers develop autonomy when they recognize that toddlers need to feel self-sufficient and capable. On the other hand, discouraging autonomy can lead to a sense of shame or doubt. Shame or doubt brings with it a range of negative feelings and inappropriate behaviors, including guilt or sadness, self-consciousness, and poor self-esteem; hesitation to try new activities; increased resistance to adult guidance; and for some children, overdependence on adults.

> *The challenge for those who care for toddlers is to find a balance between their opposite needs for dependence and independence, and for freedom and security.*

The challenge for toddlers' caregivers is to find a balance between the opposite needs for dependence and independence, and for freedom and security. On one hand, toddlers need and want to do things for themselves. On the other hand, they want and need the feeling of protection and guidance from a nurturing adult. Success in walking, learning new skills such as feeding themselves or walking up or down stairs, using a toilet, making choices, and learning to talk better all help their sense of autonomy grow.

Parents and other caregivers can support toddlers' growing sense of autonomy in small but important ways. For example, you might provide a small step stool for them in order to reach the faucet and wash their hands; hand them socks in their upright position; or place toys on low, open shelves. You can also offer them choices such as "Do you want to wear your jacket or your sweater today?"

As with other areas of development, the way adults respond to toddlers' efforts to be autonomous can either help or delay them. Relationships and interactions that are overrestrictive or overprotective, that are too permissive, or that expect behavior beyond the toddler's ability, can interfere with toddlers' developing sense of autonomy.

Sharing control with the toddler can be difficult, especially in a child care setting. Deciding when and how to provide choices is key to helping toddlers gain a sense of autonomy. Guidance and discipline techniques that do not offer choices can turn into power struggles that result in anger, frustration, and lack of cooperation.

When their sense of autonomy is stronger than their feelings of shame and doubt, toddlers more easily develop feelings of adequacy, competence, security, self-worth, and healthy self-acceptance. Children with these qualities are better able to cooperate with others and learn socially acceptable behaviors.

Attachment Behaviors

Theories of bonding and attachment have received much attention in recent years. *Bonding* refers to the strong emotional connection between the mother or father (or other caregiver) and the infant. Bonding occurs in the early days or weeks after birth. Attachment happens gradually during the first year, and it is based on the quality of the interactions between the child and the parent or other primary caregiver.

Once infants begin to form attachments, they also begin to recognize that not all caregivers are the same person. At this point, most if not all children develop a fear of strangers and *separation anxiety*. Signs include avoiding or hiding from strangers and crying when strangers are near. Separation anxiety begins to occur when the relationship between the infant and the attachment person (mother, father, or other primary caregiver) becomes more intense and exclusive.

Definition: *Separation anxiety*—the fear children have of being separated from the person to whom they are attached.

Between the ages of one and three, toddlers go through a phase of attachment called *proximity seeking*. During this time, they become very aware of their attachment person, usually their mothers. They very much want to be near and to be held by that person, and they will cry when separated. At first, toddlers will stay quite close to the person, perhaps in the adult's lap. They may cautiously move away from the attachment person, then return every once in a while for assurance. As their sense of trust and self-confidence grows, these separations gradually become longer.

Definition: *Proximity seeking*—a child's attempts to stay near or physically touch her attachment person.

As toddlers get older, they begin to be comfortable even when they can only see, hear, or talk to the attachment person. And as their feelings of security with the attachment person and with their environment grow stronger, they begin to explore even more. Soon, they can comfort themselves with behaviors such as thumb-sucking or holding a soft toy or blanket.

Forming trusting relationships and secure attachments to parents and family members are among the first and most important psychosocial tasks of infants and toddlers. As toddlers get older, they begin to form attachments outside the family. These relationships include neighbors, family friends, babysitters, and other caregivers. Successful experiences with these relationships improve the child's psychosocial development.

On the other hand, children whose first attachments are insecure come to believe that adults will not help them and cannot be trusted. Such beliefs impede their ability to form supportive relationships with other adults.

Angela's school-based child care center is excellent. The caregivers are educated in child development and early education and are warm, nurturing, and effective teachers.

Two-year-old Angela is active, alert, and eager to explore, and she has become reasonably secure at the child care center. She has developed a strong attachment to her primary caregiver, Ms. Ruiz, who has equally strong feelings for Angela.

When she arrives today, Angela looks for Ms. Ruiz. Her face shows both hope and worry. Seeing her, Angela runs to give Ms. Ruiz a big hug. Ms. Ruiz greets Angela with a wide smile and a hug, too, then offers to help Angela with her coat. Angela pulls away, however, wanting to do this herself. Ms. Ruiz reminds Angela to say good-bye to her mother, Cheryl, who must leave for algebra class. Angela watches tentatively as Cheryl leaves. Rushing to the door, she calls to her mother, who returns, kisses her good-bye, tells her to have a good time, and then goes on to class. Angela cries a little from the separation anxiety.

Ms. Ruiz sees this and directs Angela's attention to the large classroom aquarium, points to the fish, and begins to name the items in the aquarium: gravel, light, water. *She talks with Angela about the fish: "Yes, that is a fish, Angela. This one is an angelfish. Let's put some food in the aquarium for the fish." This interaction is part of each morning's routine, and, though quite short, it helps Angela to make the change from home to center and from mother to caregiver. Now feeling more relaxed, Angela says, "No more fish" and runs off to play in another part of the room, where she sees her friend, Leah.*

The child care center Jeremy attends is also excellent, and he likes go-ing there. In recent weeks, however, separation has become a particu-lar problem for him and for his parents and caregivers. There has been high staff turnover in recent months and as a result, Jeremy has had three different primary caregivers in under a year.

Unable to understand where the caregivers went and why they are suddenly gone, Jeremy is getting confused, worried, and angry. Today, he holds his mother tightly and cries. Soon, his special friend, Josh, arrives and goes to see Jeremy. Josh doesn't understand why Jeremy is crying and he isn't sure what to do. Ann says, "Hi, Josh. Jeremy, here's Josh. Josh wants to play with you." Jeremy soon stops crying. Slowly and reluctantly, he reaches toward his mother for a hug good-bye. They hug and kiss and Ann begins to lead Jeremy and Josh toward the block center. Once the two are involved, Ann says a reassuring good-bye and leaves without more problems.

These examples show that toddlers can form strong attachments with people outside the family, both adults and children, and that these attach-ments can be another source of security for toddlers. Clearly, both Angela and Jeremy feel safe in their child care center relationships. Ms. Ruiz has become a reliable and trusted source of security for Angela when she's away from her mom. Josh is now Jeremy's trusted friend, and because Josh is there every day, he is a comfort for Jeremy, especially given the changes in caregivers at the center.

Good child care offers an expanded circle of friends and healthy, supportive relationships for young children.

Good child care offers an expanded circle of friends and healthy, sup-portive relationships for young children. However, as you can see from Jeremy's situation, staff changes can create stress. Stable caregiver staff can help children develop secure attachments in out-of-home settings. Chil-dren who have many different caregivers may fail to become attached to any of them.

Social Learning and Social Cognition

According to Jean Piaget, a Swiss psychologist, toddlers are not fully ca-pable of understanding the perspectives and needs of others. As a result, they are *egocentric* (in this case, egocentric doesn't mean "selfish" but that toddlers cannot see things from another person's view). This characteristic affects both their cognitive abilities and their psychosocial development.

Toddlers' behaviors show that they believe that others feel, see, and hear the same things they do. Their inability to share is connected to this thinking and is common behavior at this stage. Toddlers may suddenly say, "Mine!" and grab a toy another child is using because they are unable to recognize that the other child may want the toy as well. Similarly, a toddler may say to his mother, who is nursing his younger sister, "Does her have a mommy?" This type of behavior shows that he can't really see past his own experiences. The three-year-old who tries to cheer up a crying nursery school friend with her own special fuzzy blanket assumes that her friend also can be comforted by this particular object. And the child who asks his grandmother over the phone, "Do you like the new shoes I have on?" does not yet understand that his grandmother cannot see through the telephone.

Although toddlers are egocentric, new research seems to show that young children may be less so than we once thought. Studies of *prosocial behaviors* and empathy in young children are changing our thinking about egocentrism in young children.

> Definition: *Prosocial behavior*—behavior that benefits others, such as helping, sharing, comforting, and defending.

Prosocial Learning and Behaviors

Fairly typical behaviors in young children include kindness, sympathy, generosity, helpfulness, and concern in the face of unfairness or cruelty. Psychologists refer to these behaviors as prosocial because they are intended to help others without the expectation of a reward. Most often, you will see prosocial behaviors in toddlers during pretend play, and they'll happen more often as toddlers have increased opportunities to interact with others. In addition, as toddlers' cognitive abilities grow, they are able to increasingly see situations from the perspectives of others, which is an important component of healthy prosocial development.

When parents and caregivers demonstrate helpfulness, unselfishness, cooperation, sympathy, and other prosocial behaviors, they provide powerful examples for toddlers, helping them develop these new behaviors.

When parents and caregivers demonstrate helpfulness, unselfishness, cooperation, sympathy, and other prosocial behaviors, they provide powerful examples for toddlers, helping them develop these new behaviors. Guidance and discipline with young children also affect the development of prosocial behaviors. Guidance that is understanding, supportive, and reasonable helps toddlers understand their culture's social expectations.

Jeremy's teacher asked him to sit by her and talk about a problem he had just had with a playmate over the use of a puzzle. Both children wanted to work on the puzzle, but not together. The teacher asked Jeremy how he thought his friend felt when he hit her. She also asked him to think about what he might do about the situation now that his friend was crying.

Toddlers need adults to help them control their impulses. An adult who says, "I can't let you hit Shannon; hitting hurts people," helps the toddler to think about the other person. This guidance should be supportive of each child in the encounter. Blaming and punishing only reinforce negative behaviors, and they do not give toddlers alternative prosocial options or help them become aware of and understand the feelings of others.

Child care professionals can help children develop prosocial behaviors by commenting on their spontaneous attempts to share, help, or cooperate: "Bobby *feels better* now that you are friends again." "That was *kind* of you to get Tamara a puzzle like yours." "That was very *helpful* of you to put the blocks away with Josh."

Such comments help in two ways: They give positive feedback and reinforcement, and provide words or names for prosocial behaviors. Having names for these actions actually helps toddlers better understand and appreciate other people's views and needs.

Moral Development

Moral behavior is the ability to think about the needs and well-being of others, and it includes such behaviors as honesty, dependability, helpfulness, and fairness. Moral individuals do not steal from others or physically hurt or emotionally abuse them. They do not betray trusts and are faithful to family, friends, and commitments.

Toddlers need a certain level of cognitive and social development, maturity, and experiences before they can develop moral reasoning, judgment, and a conscience. Young children are just beginning to develop ideas of right and wrong. Because they develop moral values through experiences and social learning opportunities, we say that infants and toddlers are *premoral*. They are guided by outside rules and expectations of obedience rather than by an inner system of values, beliefs, or understandings.

Premoral children think of "good" or "bad" in terms of doing what they are told to do. At this stage, moral behaviors (obedience) are motivated by the hope of rewards (praise and attention) or by avoiding punishment (having a toy or privilege taken away).

> Definition: *Premoral*—the time in early childhood when children are not aware of moral rules or values.

Empathy is the ability to identify with and understand another person's feelings or difficulties. It is affected by both emotional and cognitive development. Toddlers like Josh and Jeremy may respond empathetically to each other's suffering (emotional development), but they don't have enough knowledge and experience to fully understand the cause of a problem or to know what might fix it (cognitive development).

Adults need to recognize and understand the stages of moral development and the egocentric perspective of the child so that they can respond appropriately. During infancy and into the toddler period, the premoral child is incapable of evaluating the morality of her own actions or those of others. But once toddlers become aware that there are expected standards for behaving, they appear to be naturally motivated to meet them. When adult expectations conflict with toddlers' goals, toddlers will test the limits to learn which behaviors bring a reaction from adults. Adults often mistakenly think these actions are mischievous or naughty, when in fact, toddlers are only looking for information.

Embarrassing or humiliating discipline does little to help toddlers learn appropriate behaviors. In fact, many negative and socially unacceptable behaviors, as well as low self-esteem, grow out of inappropriate discipline techniques.

By age two, children are fairly aware of their parents' "do's and don'ts" and generally obey them when their parents are near. The ability to follow such rules when their parents are absent does not come until around age three.

During this stage, adults can teach proper behaviors as opportunities arise. When, for example, a toddler grabs a toy from another child or bites to defend himself, the caregiver can use these opportunities to guide the child toward more appropriate behaviors. Guidance that punishes rather than provides intelligent, logical instruction fails to recognize that moral behaviors grow out of understanding and prosocial learning (perspective taking, empathy, unselfishness, and so on). Embarrassing or humiliating discipline does little to help toddlers learn appropriate behaviors. In fact, many negative and socially unacceptable behaviors, as well as low self-esteem, grow out of inappropriate discipline techniques.

Keep in mind, too, that moral development happens throughout life. Social learning occurs in many situations with many different people in the course of a lifetime. Your goal as a caregiver is to help children become adults whose sense of morality is based within them, rather than on outside rules and the threat of punishment.

A Neurological Development Perspective on Psychosocial Growth

A child's early years are critical, particularly for the neurological development that is connected to attachment, the control of emotions, and the ability to cope with stress. The human brain grows and develops first in its lower, more primitive parts (brain stem and midbrain) and then its higher regions (limbic and cortical). As the brain grows and develops, the areas of higher intelligence begin to influence or control the more primitive behaviors coming from the lower regions of the brain. The way in which toddlers, school-age children, and adults each react to frustration, for example, *should* be quite different because the structures of their brains are quite different.

The structure and function of our developing brains are determined by experiences, particularly early interpersonal relationships.

For example, toddlers often show frustration with a tantrum (coming from lower brain regions). School-age children usually control their impulse to act out and use words to express needs and emotions or even ask another child or an adult for help (cortical functions, coming from the higher brain regions). Older children and adults are able to evaluate a frustrating situation (again, a cortical function). As the upper regions of the brain become organized, humans gain the ability to control or alter lower brain activity such as aggression, impulsiveness, and hyperactivity.

The structure and function of our developing brains are determined by experiences, particularly early interpersonal relationships. As toddlers repeatedly interact with the people they are attached to, their brains form important neurological connections that will function in positive or negative ways, depending on the types and number of experiences they have with their attachment people and early caregivers (Siegel 1999).

When young children's family experiences don't support healthy brain development, their brains can actually fail to develop impulse-controlling abilities. When children experience ongoing maltreatment and stress, their brains stay in a state of heightened arousal and fight-or-flight preparedness that stimulates the brain stem. As a result, the lower region of the child's brain, which is responsible for innate urges such as aggression and impulsivity, is in a state of high activity. At the same time, when infants and toddlers don't have warm, nurturing relationships that reassure and protect them, the ability of the higher brain structures to regulate these urges is decreased. Aggression and violence have their origins in these disruptions.

In chapter 6, we examined theories of toddlers' psychosocial development, including their need to be both independent and dependent of their caregivers; the emergence of prosocial and moral learning; and the connection to toddlers' brain development. In chapter 7, you'll learn about the important factors that affect psychosocial development in children ages one through three, beginning with the social interactions and play behaviors. Young children today spend a great deal of time in out-of-home child care, and you'll learn what effect this has on their development. You'll also learn about the common fears and worries toddlers have and what they do to comfort themselves. You'll find fascinating and useful information on the development of self-concept and self-esteem, and how awareness of gender, racial, and individual differences develop.

Reference

Siegel, D. J. 1999. *The developing mind: Toward a neurobiology of interpersonal experience*. New York: Guilford Press.

7 Dimensions of Psychosocial Development

Temperament

From birth, infants have unique personalities, his or her own way of feeling, thinking, and interacting with others. *Temperament* is the term generally used to describe this uniqueness. Researchers Stella Chess and Alexander Thomas (1987, 1996) have identified three main types of temperament:

1. *The easy temperament.* These children are usually easygoing, even-tempered, accepting of change, playful, open, and adaptable. Their eating and sleeping schedules are quite regular, they are easily comforted when upset, and they generally are in a good mood.

2. *The difficult temperament.* These children are slower to develop regular eating and sleeping routines, are more irritable, get less pleasure from playtime activities, have difficulty adjusting to changes in routines, and tend to cry louder and longer than more easily soothed children.

3. *The slow-to-warm-up temperament.* These children show only mild positive or negative reactions; they don't like new situations and new people; they are moody and slow to adapt. The slow-to-warm-up child may resist close interactions such as cuddling.

Although temperament may be genetically determined, it is also affected by the environment the child grows up in. Think of your brothers, sisters, cousins, or other relatives. What are the similarities and differences in their temperaments?

James, Angela's father, is low-key and affectionate. He enjoys holding Angela on his lap, and talking and reading books with her. His manner has a calming effect on Angela, and she asks him to hold her the moment he arrives for a visit. Knowing that he enjoys reading to her, Angela runs off to get a book—any book—to offer to him.

Angela is outgoing, affectionate, observant, and talkative; she loves to name the people and objects in her house. Though she can't focus her attention for more than a few minutes, she seems to need and enjoy the long interactions with James and the books they share. Angela has learned how to get and hold her father's attention. Her developing sense of autonomy, along with her temperament, are blending with the temperament and personality of her father.

Cheryl is more physically active with Angela. She likes to chase Angela around the house, play hide-and-seek, take her on outings, walk around the neighborhood with her, and dance and sing with her. They especially enjoy playing copycat games with each other. Angela has learned when and how to interest her mother in these playful times, which make both of them very happy.

James and Cheryl relate to Angela in different ways; they each bring their unique personalities and skills. Their interactions with Angela are different, yet complementary.

Social Interactions and Play Behaviors

Young children today spend more time in out-of-home child care situations than children of past generations did. As a result many infants and toddlers today have met and played with other children from a very early age.

In child care and other settings, first attempts at interaction are often clumsy and sometimes even a bit hostile. Eventually, toddler friends begin to imitate one another, laugh with and at one another, follow one another around, and share activities, such as looking at books together or filling and dumping objects from a container. Although these relationships may be brief, they are an obvious first step in learning to make and keep friendships. Very young children can become attached to one another at an early age, and their play is more focused and successful when they are with children they have known for some time.

One study found that when infants and toddlers were moved to a new classroom, they were able to adapt much more quickly when a close friend was moved with them. Today, many programs use staffing patterns that move the caregiver or teacher to the next age or grade level with a class of children in order to maintain the connection and security of relationships for those children.

Studies of toddler friendships and play behaviors show that they often engage in *parallel play*. In parallel play, a toddler will enjoy being near and playing beside another child, but is involved in her own activity. Little if any interaction occurs between the two children. Researchers previously thought that parallel play happened only in the early stages of social development, but more recent studies have shown that while parallel play is quite common in the toddler years, it is not limited to that period and can take on different forms with increasing cognitive and social skill development.

> *Young children today spend more time in out-of-home child care situations than children of past generations did; as a result, they've met and played with other children from a very early age.*

Fears and Anxieties during the Toddler Period

As you have already learned, separation and stranger anxiety are normal parts of the toddler period. These worries are the result of toddlers' increasing cognitive abilities as well as their attachment to parents and other caregivers. (Fortunately, they begin to lessen around age two-and-a-half to three.)

But young toddlers (around eighteen months) have other fears too. As a result of their growing cognitive abilities, children this age are now able to manipulate mental images, formulate ideas, and think about past events and experiences. But their ability to imagine often lacks the ability to tell the difference between real and unreal. These new thoughts, as well as the misunderstandings and misconceptions that come along with them, can lead to new fears.

Toddlers' fears are normal. They are very real to them and thus can be very disturbing and difficult to calm. In addition to fear of separation and strangers, toddlers commonly fear the dark, the bathtub drain, animals, some storybook or media characters, monsters and ghosts, lightning and thunder, and vacuum cleaners or other noisy equipment.

Helping them understand and cope with fear requires sensitivity and patience. Because toddlers' fears are so real to them, caregivers should never laugh at, ridicule, or minimize them. Very young children will not understand logical explanations; instead, toddlers need adults to help them find ways to deal with their fears. A child who is afraid of the bathtub drain, for instance, can be given "control" over it by being the one who opens or closes the drain or by getting out of the tub before the drain is opened.

Fears are necessary for survival, of course, because they tell us that danger is near. While toddlers may develop a number of other fears during this time, they do not have many of the survival fears necessary for dangerous situations. They don't have the judgment, the experience, or the understanding to avoid such hazards as street crossings, fire, poisons, heights, guns, and many other dangers in their environments.

Toddlers need to be protected with close supervision. They must be taught in ways that give them knowledge, caution, and skills, but without frightening them too much. Adults must set limits and rules that both protect and teach toddlers and must recognize that with toddlers, reminders are needed regularly.

Self-Comforting Behaviors

When frightened, lonely, sad, tired, bored, or trying to relax or fall asleep, infants and toddlers often use special—and sometimes unusual—self-comforting behaviors. These self-comforting behaviors help children cope with their emotions and include thumb-sucking or attachment to a toy, piece of clothing or blanket (called a *transitional object*).

Most infants find their fists and thumbs sooner or later and get much pleasure and comfort from sucking on them. Child development researchers now say that parents should expect their infants and toddlers to suck their thumbs, fingers, or fists and should not worry because there are few consequences to this behavior.

> Definition: *Transitional object*—an object, usually soft and cuddly, to which a child becomes attached.

Attachment to a transitional object, such as a teddy bear, special blanket, swatch of soft fabric, doll, or favorite piece of clothing, is common and usually begins around eight or nine months. Because these objects have certain meanings and bring out comforting feelings, toddlers become emotionally attached to them. This connection can last to age seven or eight and sometimes beyond. Such objects can help toddlers ease anxiety and give them security in stressful situations.

Self-Concept and Self-Esteem

Self-concept is the definition we form of ourselves. It means that we are aware of ourselves as separate, unique individuals. Toddlers' self-concepts grow out of their interactions with others, how they understand those interactions, and their ability to accept or ignore the positive or negative feedback they perceive in those interactions. Essentially, toddlers devise their self-concept from the way parents, teachers, other adults and other children relate to them.

The self-concept is dynamic. It changes over time with additional experiences and with increasing physical/motor, social, and cognitive abilities. Generally, the development of the self-concept consists of four accomplishments: self-awareness, self-recognition, self-definition, and self-esteem.

Self-awareness develops as infants begin to realize that they are separate from other people and that objects are not part of them. *Self-recognition* refers to infants' ability to recognize themselves in a mirror, photograph, or drawing. This ability seems to come at the same time that they can form and hold mental images—usually by eighteen months of age. Most children can recognize a photograph of themselves by age two.

Self-definition appears as children begin to use language to describe themselves. Toddlers' growing awareness of their age, size, gender, and skills help them with this definition. When young children take pride in telling you how old they are, self-definition has begun. Holding up three fingers and saying, "I am three," is an attempt to define oneself. When children ask for attention by saying, "Watch me!" they are demonstrating the skills by which they define themselves. "I can reach it," "Watch me jump," and "I am big," are other indications of emerging self-concept.

Around age three, children begin to mentally construct an "autobiographical" memory. Eventually it will be a continuous identity they carry throughout life. This memory of one's experiences, emotions, and personality depends very much on the types of interactions and relationships infants and toddlers have had with their early caregivers. It also influences the development of positive self-esteem.

Self-esteem emerges from the feedback young children receive from others and how they perceive that feedback. Children who see themselves as loved, valued, worthy, and competent develop healthy self-esteem. Children who receive negative responses from their caregivers, such as punishment, abuse, or neglect, develop lower self-esteem.

Children who see themselves as loved, valued, worthy, and competent develop healthy self-esteem.

An interesting part of self-definition begins when children begin to "self-correct." Coloring over a drawing to "cover it up," throwing an art project into the trash because "it doesn't look right," starting over on simple tasks, and other similar behaviors show that a child is beginning to look at herself. These behaviors show that the child wants to succeed. Through such actions, children begin to feel the emotions of pride, shame, embarrassment, or guilt. A child with healthy self-esteem will generally feel more positive than negative about the process.

Gender Awareness

As stated previously, most children know whether they are a boy or a girl by age two-and-a-half to three. During the second year of toddlers' lives, parents and other caregivers begin to see differences in the way boys and girls play. These differences tend to be stereotypical, and they may be caused by gender-based experiences provided by the parents. For example, parents may be more gentle and cuddling with girls and more rough and tumble with boys, or they may talk more tenderly to girls and more directly to boys. At this age boys and girls may also begin to play with different kinds of toys—boys tend to play with transportation toys, blocks, and other things they can manipulate, while girls typically choose soft toys and dolls, and enjoy dressing up and dancing. However, these play choices may simply reflect the types of toys parents have provided for their boys or girls.

At the same time, it is not unusual for toddlers to think that their gender can change, that is, that boys can grow up to become mothers and girls can grow up to be fathers. This thinking shows that toddlers have not yet developed a sense of *gender constancy*. Young children do not usually fully understand the idea of gender constancy until ages five to seven.

Definition: *Gender constancy*—the realization that a person's gender remains the same, regardless of age or changes in clothing, hairstyles, or other outward characteristics.

Psychologists and educators now encourage less gender stereotyping of children's early experiences, whether with books, toys, entertainment media, or adult expectations. Boys can certainly be allowed to show feelings, to nurture and be nurtured, and to participate in a range of activities from gentle to rough. Girls can be encouraged to try physical activities and to be more assertive.

Awareness of Diversity and Individual Differences

How do children become aware of and respond to racial differences? Toddlers primarily focus on people's outward features. Young children notice facial features: skin color; hair color, texture, and style; clothing; and voice and speech patterns. They do not, however, develop any awareness of race until ages three to eight. Mature forms of racial awareness, which do not rely on superficial features but on deeper understandings of ethnicity, do not appear until age nine or ten.

Toddlers' primary source of information about race is the family, where racial attitudes are passed on and racial pride is developed and encouraged. Children learn about similarities and differences among people through their experiences with others outside their immediate family as well as through their toys, books, and the media. In recent years, racial groups have been portrayed more accurately in children's books, toys, school curricula, and the media. Nevertheless, child care professionals still need to check these sources to guarantee accurate, positive, and non-biased views. The toddler's racial identity and attitudes toward people of other races and ethnic groups depend on accurate information and sensitive guidance.

Development of Self-Control

While developing self-control is an important early childhood psychosocial goal, it is not one that will be met quickly. For the most part, self-control is a learned behavior and takes many years. It depends on external controls at first, such as rules set by parents and other caregivers. As the years pass, children gradually take more and more responsibility for their behaviors. In very young children, this process is neither fast nor smooth. Indicators of self-control in children include:

- control of impulses
- tolerance of frustration
- the ability to postpone immediate satisfaction
- the ability to create a project and finish it over a period of time (Marion 2003)

As with other areas of psychosocial development, cognition and social experiences both play a role in the development of self-control. Adults can help toddlers develop better self-control by using developmentally appropriate teaching and guidance.

Below you will find effective suggestions that teachers and other child care professionals can use to help toddlers develop self-control.

HELPING YOUNG CHILDREN DEVELOP SELF-CONTROL

1. Provide an environment in which the child's growing sense of autonomy can grow; this includes the following:
   a. play items
   b. experiences that are interesting and enriching
   c. low, open shelves for personal and play items
   d. adequate space for use, storage, and retrieval of personal and play items
   e. safe and sturdy furnishings and toys
   f. placement of dangerous and off-limits items out of sight and out of reach (or under lock and key, as appropriate)
2. Provide an atmosphere that encourages toddlers to make choices, explore, and discover, as long as it also fits their developmental stage and ability, and is free of pressure to perform.
3. Provide a daily schedule that is predictable so that toddlers can sense the day's rhythms and anticipate and respond appropriately to regular events, such as mealtimes, bath time, nap time, story time, and so on.
4. Set logical, reasonable, and fair limits for behavior; then consistently and predictably enforce them. Use words and explanations rather than punishment to help toddlers understand these limits.
5. Quickly meet the toddler's needs for food, clothing, rest, and attention. Toddlers have trouble waiting for what they need and do not tolerate frustration well.

Toddler Mental Health

Ongoing and rapid development during the toddler period brings about dramatic changes in physiological, emotional, social, and cognitive characteristics. You can see these growth-related changes in the behaviors that continually confuse and frustrate toddlers' caregivers, such as mood changes, negativity, not doing what is expected, tantrums, power struggles, rejecting affection, aggression, and eating and sleeping difficulties.

Most of these behaviors are perfectly normal; in fact, many of them are signs of a maturing and healthy child. There is reason for concern, however, when primary caregivers' personalities and needs conflict with the toddler's capabilities and needs. Professional intervention may be required. The goal is to resolve the issues before they get deeper and additional behavior problems appear, such as withdrawal, hostility, or prolonged sadness or depression.

Factors Influencing Psychosocial Development

Recognizing the factors that affect toddlers' psychosocial development during the toddler period helps adults to provide essential and appropriate experiences. The best possible psychosocial development depends on these earliest experiences.

QUALITY OF ATTACHMENTS

Children in every culture form attachments to their caregivers. This serves their basic needs for comfort and protection. Scholars believe that infants' first attachments have a lifelong influence on their physical well-being, personality development, mental health, social relationships, and moral behaviors. Toddlers continue to need the closeness, protection, emotional support, and social interaction that a loving and caring attachment person provides.

SUPPORT AND ENCOURAGEMENT OF A SENSE OF AUTONOMY

How parents and caregivers respond to toddlers' needs for autonomy is critical. Toddlers want to be independent, but at the same time they very much need a safe, secure relationship that allows them to be dependent too. Helping toddlers balance these opposite needs is difficult. Parents and other caregivers must understand how important it is for toddlers to get through this developmental crisis successfully.

TEMPERAMENT

Each child's unique temperament and personality affect other people and are affected by other people. The quality and number of early interactions either support or harm the child's emerging sense of self and self-esteem.

GUIDANCE AND DISCIPLINE TECHNIQUES

Guidance and discipline techniques that are consistent, predictable, logical, and supportive help toddlers begin to develop self-control, perspective, and increasing competence in social interactions. Toddlers need guidelines that nurture their growing independence while recognizing their continuing need for reasonable rules, clear limits, and constant protection. In addition, through positive, instructive, and supportive interactions with adults, toddlers begin to learn to recognize, express, and deal with emotions.

OPPORTUNITIES TO LEARN THROUGH SOCIAL INTERACTIONS

Interactions with siblings and other children their age give toddlers the social experiences that help them understand social rules and the feelings and intentions of others. Although friendships between toddlers are awkward and often temporary, they help toddlers begin to understand the difference between themselves and others.

QUALITY OF PLAY EXPERIENCES

Appropriate and satisfying play with other children and developmentally appropriate toys and games encourage psychosocial growth in many ways: physical/motor, cognitive, language, reading, and social and moral skills. Play improves toddlers' language ability, which, in turn, increases their ability to tell others what their needs are, to understand new concepts, and to solve problems. Play introduces toddlers to social rules—another step in learning how to control their own behavior. Through play, toddlers experiment with a variety of social roles and emerging social skills, and continue to learn about expressing emotions. Play helps them resolve a number of fears and anxieties and, in doing so, supports their sense of competence.

SOCIAL LEARNING IN MANY CONTEXTS

Experiences both within the family and in a variety of social situations help children learn to appreciate that they are unique and that every other person is unique, too. Racial awareness also begins in these early years. Self-esteem, family pride, acceptance, and respect for others develop and grow in the home and in child care settings where nonbiased curricula are available.

SUPPORT FOR SPECIAL DEVELOPMENTAL NEEDS

Although we have not specifically discussed children with special needs in this chapter, it is important to note that children with delayed development, chronic disease, or disabilities are especially in need of healthy, supportive emotional and social interactions. Because these children depend so much on long-term attachment behaviors, their fears, anxieties, frustrations, and disappointments as well as their developing senses of autonomy, social competence, self-concept development, and healthy self-esteem are at risk. Adults must be particularly sensitive to these children's needs for help and encouragement in social situations as well as opportunities to develop autonomy. Adults may need to teach and model effective social interaction.

References

Chess, S., and A. Thomas. 1987. *Origins and evolution of behavior disorders from infancy to early adult life.* Cambridge, Mass.: Harvard University Press.

———. 1996. *Temperament: Theory and practice.* New York: Brunner/Mazel.

Marion, M. 2003. *Guidance of young children.* 6th ed. Upper Saddle River, N.J.: Prentice Hall.

The Role of the Early Childhood Professional

1. Recognize the very important role adults have in directing psychosocial development in young children.
2. Understand the toddler's egocentric perspective.
3. Help toddlers develop autonomy by providing safe surroundings, reasonable limits, opportunities to make choices, and thoughtful help as needed.
4. Provide positive, predictable, supportive, and educational guidance.
5. Understand toddlers' continuing dependency and need for security and protection.
6. Encourage play opportunities with other children.
7. Provide names for emotions and help toddlers learn how to express them.
8. Promote self-esteem through positive, supportive interactions and with sensitive, accurate responses to questions about race and gender.
9. Provide developmentally appropriate and age-appropriate books, toys, and electronic media that increase toddlers' understanding of themselves and of others.
10. Learn to observe and respond to toddlers' signals and clues.

Discussion Questions

1. List some examples of simple, age-appropriate self-help tasks for toddlers. What modifications can you make to your physical setting to help alleviate frustrations as toddlers go about completing such tasks? Could you, for example, provide low coat hooks near cubbies so that toddlers could hang up their own coats? What supervised daily tasks might you invite toddlers to participate in that would help them gain autonomy and boost their confidence? For example, could they help set the table for lunch or be asked to "read" a book to a younger child while you prepare snack?
2. Come up with some daily rituals you might add to your routines and transitions that would foster children's sense of security and trust. What methods or rituals do you currently use in your program to promote bonding with the children and lessen separation anxiety?
3. Write down some examples of prosocial behavior you have seen toddlers practicing. Based on the discussion of prosocial learning in chapter 6, what activities could you introduce to encourage prosocial learning in your setting?
4. How do you introduce the concepts of similarity and difference to the toddlers in your program? If your program is not very culturally diverse, how might you begin to teach toddlers to respect others who look or talk differently than they do? If your program is culturally di-

verse, how do you show respect for the differing beliefs and practices of the families in your program? Make a plan for addressing these issues.

Further Reading

Bronson, M. B. 2000. *Self-regulation in early childhood: Nature and nurture.* New York: Guilford Press.

Denham, S. A. 1998. *Emotional development in young children.* New York: Guilford Press.

Fenchel, E., ed. 2001. "Babies, toddlers and the media." *Zero to three* 22:2.

Goulet, M. 1999. *How caring relationships support self-regulation.* Washington, D.C.: National Association for the Education of Young Children.

Koplow, L. 1996. *Unsmiling faces: How preschools can heal.* New York: Teachers College Press.

Marion, M. 2003. *Guidance of young children.* 6th ed. Upper Saddle River, N.J.: Prentice Hall.

Siegel, D. J. 1999. *The developing mind: Toward a neurobiology of interpersonal experience.* New York: Guilford Press.

Other Resources

- American Academy of Pediatrics brochures:
  Toilet training: Guidelines for parents and childcare professionals
  Discipline and your child: Guidelines for parents
  Temper tantrums: A normal part of growing up

- National Association for the Education of Young Children brochures:
  Helping children learn self-control: A guide to discipline
  Love and learn: Discipline for young children
  A caring place for your infants
  A caring place for your toddler
  A good preschool for your child

Part Three

Cognitive, Language, and Literacy Development

Using their sensorimotor capacities and their abilities to master first-order symbol systems, young children develop a vast array of intuitive understandings even before they enter school. Specifically, they develop robust and functional theories of matter, life, the minds of other individuals, and their own minds and selves. They are aided in this task of theory construction by various constraints, some built into the genome, and others a function of the particular circumstances of their culture, and still others a reflection of their own, more idiosyncratic styles and inclinations.

—HOWARD GARDNER

Physical, motor, and psychosocial growth during the toddler years is both remarkable and exciting, and the changes we see during this time in toddlers' cognitive development—the part of growth that involves perception, thinking, attention, memory, problem solving, creativity, language, and literacy—are equally dramatic. In what seems to be a sudden transformation, toddlers are now beginning to use mental symbols and images in their thinking, and their ability to absorb and use language grows in leaps and bounds. Their relationships with other toddlers and their caregivers take on new dimensions as their ability to interact with and understand their world expands. Toddlers' experiences with print—in books, on billboards, on cereal boxes, and so on—set the stage for reading and writing.

In part 3, you'll learn about the interaction among thought, language, and the development of reading and writing abilities. As a child care professional, understanding what is happening physically, mentally, and emotionally for toddlers at this stage will help you enormously in your work with these children—and will let you avoid some typical pitfalls and frustrations too. You'll examine the major factors influencing toddlers' cognitive, language, and literacy development and important strategies for supporting this growth.

In the following chapters, we will look at some theories of cognitive development. At this stage of development, toddlers are apt to form illogical and incomplete conclusions about the world around them. Understanding how toddlers think can help you as a caregiver to lessen or prevent some of the problems that come with these typical misperceptions. Other topics include the multiple-intelligence theory and its significance for child care professionals, how language develops, the effects of growing up in a bilingual setting, and the interaction between thinking and language. You'll also learn how new research has greatly changed the ideas of child development experts on how and when children can learn to read, and you'll discover the steps child care professionals can take to encourage and facilitate early reading behaviors.

8 Theories of Cognitive Development

Two models of cognitive development in young children continue to dominate the early childhood field: Jean Piaget's stages theory and Howard Gardner's multiple-intelligence theory. Recent discoveries in the neurobiology of brain development have also contributed to a more sophisticated understanding of how toddlers' thinking, including their language and literacy skills, evolves.

Theories of Cognitive Development

Between ages one and two, children are still in the sensorimotor period of cognitive development, according to child development expert Jean Piaget. Born in Switzerland in 1896, Piaget established what is now considered the most famous theory of cognitive development. His studies have dominated the fields of child study, psychology, philosophy, and education since the 1920s.

One of Piaget's most important ideas was that young children think and solve problems quite differently than older children and adults do. He theorized that there are four major stages of cognitive development: the *sensorimotor period* (birth to age two), the *preoperational period* (ages two to seven), the *concrete operations period* (ages seven to eleven), and the *formal operations period* (age eleven and beyond). According to Piaget, cognitive development happens one stage at a time. He believed, too, that one stage always follows another in the same way and that each stage builds on the accomplishments of the one before it. Every child goes through these stages, but at her own speed. As a caregiver, it is important to understand the sequence of these stages so that you can respond to and interact with infants and young children in ways that will most help their cognitive development. (For more information about Piaget's stages of development, see the first book in this series, *Understanding Infant Development*, page 63.)

As children progress from infancy into the toddler period, some dramatic changes in cognitive abilities begin to take place. In their first year of life, infants rely mostly on *sensorimotor learning* as the guiding force behind their cognitive development. But as children move into their second year, they begin to rely on something new and much more complex: mental symbols and images, and conversations with others.

> Definition: *Sensorimotor learning*—learning that happens through the senses and physical activities.

At this stage, toddlers try new ways to achieve goals. They become even more curious and want to experiment. They regularly imitate others, especially their adult caregivers, and they develop a better sense of object permanence. At this stage, children are beginning to recognize cause and effect, and they are beginning to solve problems in their minds without the aid of objects or trial and error. The following vignette shows how Jeremy uses both old and new techniques to reach a goal:

> *Jeremy tries to place a triangular shape into its corresponding opening in a three-dimensional puzzle. The puzzle slips, and Jeremy misses the opening. He immediately sets the puzzle upright and holds it with one hand while using the other hand to put the piece into the opening. Jeremy's ability to set the puzzle upright and hold it with one hand shows that he has learned how to work out various problems by playing with many objects during the sensorimotor stage. He uses this new knowledge to help him reach his goal of putting the puzzle piece through the opening.*

At this time, toddlers begin to develop a sense of confidence in the permanence of objects, including people. According to Piaget, children in this stage of cognitive development realize that objects and people have an identity of their own and that they continue to exist even when they cannot be seen or heard. True object permanence means that toddlers can look for objects that they did not see being hidden.

This new understanding of object permanence can also be seen in toddlers' imitation behaviors. During this stage, children imitate not only events and behaviors in their immediate experience, but also behaviors that they've seen at other times. For example, Angela, who is eighteen months old now, picks up the remote control for the TV and pretends that she is talking on the phone. She does this even though she hasn't seen anyone talking on the phone for some hours.

THE PREOPERATIONAL STAGE

By the end of the sensorimotor period, children generally understand that objects, people, and events have certain basic characteristics, and they can hold thoughts of people, objects, and events in their minds. These new abilities, together with their increasing use of symbols through gestures, language, and play, help toddlers move into Piaget's next period of cognitive development: that of preoperational intelligence. The preoperational stage of cognitive development extends from ages two to seven.

According to Piaget, "preoperational" children are not capable of operational (logical) thinking. His studies suggest that this preoperational thinking is not just the result of lack of experience or immaturity, but rather that young children's thinking processes are actually quite different from those of older children and adults.

In table 8.1, you'll see a summary of thinking patterns of toddlers.

Table 8.1: **The Thinking of Young Children**

Characteristics of Early Childhood Thinking and Learning
Depends on sensory experiences
Is limited to what children see and experience in the world around them
Is egocentric; children don't have the ability to see the world from the perspective of other people
Relies on language and labels for the construction of meaning
Relies on prior experiences to understand new experiences
Benefits from repetition
Is beginning to understand the concepts of cause and effect
Has trouble organizing and expressing thoughts
Has trouble organizing and retelling events
Is impulsive
Confuses fantasy and reality
Is quite literal
Appears illogical to older children and adults

Young, preoperational children continue to develop the ability to use *mental symbols* in the form of gestures, language, dramatic play, and dreams. Notice how Jeremy uses mental imagery, or symbols:

Jeremy has seen city sanitation workers collecting trash around his neighborhood on his walks with his mother. One day, after seeing this for several weeks, he begins to dump all his toys on his bunk bed. Between loads, he presses the bolts at the end of his bed to "grind up the trash."

Adults often describe the thinking and statements of preoperational toddlers as "cute," "funny," or "strange." These comments seem humorous because toddlers are forming conclusions based on illogical or incomplete ideas. This happens because toddlers can focus attention on only a few aspects of an object or experience, and sometimes they're the least important ones.

When Angela, at age two and a half, was asked by her dad, "What do you want to be when you grow up?" she answered, "Nothing."

"Why do you say nothing?" her dad asked. "Isn't there something you want to be?"

Angela answered, "No, Angela no car. Need car for work."

Angela has focused her attention on the fact that grown-ups drive cars to work. Therefore, she can't imagine what she can be or do when she is grown, since she can't drive right now. Jeremy's comments also show typical toddler reasoning.

Jeremy and his parents are visiting relatives for the holidays. After dinner, Jeremy's Aunt Sarah gives the children their gifts. Sarah spent approximately equal amounts of money on the children, careful not to favor one child over another. However, Jeremy's three-year-old cousin, Matthew, receives several presents, while Jeremy is given only one. As a typical preoperational child, Jeremy notices only the number of presents, not their value, because the idea of value is outside his understanding. Jeremy is therefore upset, because his cousin "gots more presents."

At this age, toddlers' thinking is strongly affected by their perceptions, which are dominated by how things seem. Understanding how young children think can help any caregiver lessen or prevent the problems that come with these typical misperceptions.

Another characteristic of preoperational thinking is overgeneralizing personal experiences to other situations or experiences. Here's an example:

At three years old, Jeremy was waking at night with dreams of ghosts and monsters. In her child care training, Jeremy's babysitter, Phyllis, had learned that young children blend fantasy with reality. She knew that Jeremy's dreams were real to him. For this reason, she did not say, "Jeremy, there are no ghosts or monsters. They are pretend." Instead, she comforted him and reassured him that she and his parents were there at night to keep him safe. Phyllis told Jeremy that they would not let the ghosts and monsters hurt him.

As the disturbing dreams continued for several more weeks, Phyllis got an idea. She asked Jeremy what he thought could be done to keep the ghosts and monsters out of his room. Jeremy thought for a moment and then said, "Make a sign. 'Ghosts and monsters keep out.'" Phyllis got some paper and crayons and helped Jeremy draw a sign with that message. She and Jeremy then put the sign on his door.

Jeremy used his past experience with signs to solve his problem. Phyllis did not impose adult problem solving and reasoning on Jeremy, but instead let him solve his problem in a way that made sense to him. Bill, Ann, and Phyllis remind Jeremy at bedtime that they are there to keep him safe and that there is a sign on his door telling the monsters and ghosts to keep out. During the next few weeks, Jeremy's sleep is more peaceful.

> *Preoperational children are not selfish, they're egocentric; that is, they can't look at objects or situations from another's perspective.*

Piaget described preoperational children as egocentric. However, as we noted in chapter 6, *egocentrism* doesn't mean that children are selfish; instead, it means that children aren't able to look at objects or situations from another's perspective. Toddlers' perspectives are based on their own limited experiences, and, as a result, they aren't able to think about the thoughts and feelings of others. Piaget suggested that through interactions with other children and adults, egocentric thought becomes more socialized.

Angela's teacher takes the three-year-olds outdoors to play. Angela and two other children begin to play in the sand pile. Angela grabs a sifter from one of the children. This child stares at Angela and then leaves the sand area. After several minutes, Angela tries to take a large bucket from another child, Cedrick. He firmly grasps the bucket and refuses to let her have it. Angela then begins hitting Cedrick, who runs crying to the teacher. The teacher calmly asks

Cedrick what happened. Cedrick takes her hand and leads her to the sand pile, telling her that Angela took his bucket and hit him. Angela's teacher asks Cedrick to tell Angela why he was crying, and the teacher repeats to Angela what Cedrick tells her. Calmly and objectively, the teacher describes the consequences of Angela's behavior. "Angela hit Cedrick. Hitting hurts. Cedrick feels bad and is crying. He said he had the bucket first. Here is another big bucket for you, Angela. We have lots of big buckets in our sand pile."

Angela's teacher understood that egocentric behavior is normal for three-year-olds. For that reason, she didn't tell Angela that she was a "bad girl" for hitting Cedrick. Instead, she repeated what Cedrick said, describing Angela's behavior and the consequences of her actions.

The teachers at this center also have many duplicate materials. They know that children at this age can be easily frustrated if they see and want something another child has. Having multiple materials can prevent the interruption in children's activities and can promote problem-solving skills. When it is not possible to duplicate materials, teachers can encourage more appropriate behavior by verbalizing children's concerns. For example, the teacher might say to Angela, "Cedrick said he had the big bucket first. He still wants to use it. When he is done, Cedrick will give it to you." The teacher can then watch to be sure Cedrick actually shares the bucket with Angela.

Angela is playing in the center of her classroom. She dumps plastic fruit out of a wooden bowl. As she turns the bowl over, it now seems like it could be a hat. Angela takes the bowl and with considerable force, places it on Maria's head—and Maria begins to cry. Angela looks very surprised at Maria's reaction. She pats Maria and tries to comfort her. Angela's teacher, Ms. Ruiz, noticed this interaction, and tells Maria that Angela did not mean to hurt her. Ms. Ruiz puts Maria on her lap to calm her. Angela sees Maria and then goes to her cubby, grabs her special blanket, and gives it to Maria.

Seeing other preoperational toddlers show compassion like this has made teachers, parents, and researchers alike question Piaget's idea of egocentrism. Angela's behavior seems to show that she felt sorry for Maria. She

74

tried to comfort her through gentle patting and bringing her the blanket. A number of studies have shown that under certain conditions, young children are not completely egocentric. Researchers have found that young children are better able to understand how others feel or see a situation from another person's perspective when they are presented with a problem or situation that is familiar to them. Using such familiar props as a toy police officer, Grover from *Sesame Street*, a car, boats, and animals, 88 percent of three-year-olds in a study were able to see another's point of view (Hughes and Donaldson 1983). Perhaps we need to reexamine some of our beliefs about children's responses.

Howard Gardner's Multiple-Intelligence Theory

In the last few decades, a fascinating new view of intelligence has become widely accepted in the field of education. The *multiple-intelligence theory*, proposed by contemporary scholar Howard Gardner, has had important implications for child care professionals, teachers, and parents alike.

Gardner believes that intelligence is the ability to solve problems or create a product that is valued by one's culture or community. He describes the learning of very young children as intuitive rather than rational or logical. Most important, he suggests the following:

- There are many different kinds of minds.
- We learn, remember, understand, and perform in many different ways.
- We are capable of knowing things in different ways.

In his multiple-intelligence theory, Gardner proposes that we have at least ten different "intelligences":

1. *Intrapersonal intelligence:* the ability to detect and symbolize complex and very different sets of feelings
2. *Interpersonal intelligence:* the ability to recognize distinctions among other people's moods, temperaments, motivations, and intentions
3. *Spatial intelligence:* the ability to accurately see the world
4. *Bodily kinesthetic intelligence:* the ability to direct one's bodily motions and manipulate objects skillfully
5. *Musical intelligence:* exceptional awareness of pitch, rhythm, and timbre
6. *Linguistic intelligence:* sensitivity to meaning, order, sounds, rhythms, and inflections of words

75

7. *Logical–mathematical intelligence:* the ability to attend to patterns, categories, and relationships
8. *Naturalist intelligence:* the ability to recognize important differences in the natural world among plants and animals, natural phenomena, and changes over time
9. *Spiritual intelligence:* the ability to relate to the mysteries of life and death and to the "why" questions of human existence, the supernatural, and altered states of consciousness
10. *Existential intelligence:* a part of spiritual intelligence that includes the ability to locate oneself within the cosmos—the infinite—while dealing with such intellectual issues as the meaning of life and death, the ultimate fate of the physical and psychological worlds, or other mysterious or powerful life experiences

Gardner believes that all of us have each of these kinds of intelligence in various combinations and to greater or lesser amounts. He suggests that teachers and other caregivers should not ask "How smart are you?" but rather "In what ways are you smart?" Rather than focusing only on intellectual potential, his approach emphasizes individual strengths and uniqueness. It also gives us a better idea of individual capabilities than traditional intelligence tests might give.

> *We should not ask "How smart are you?" but rather "In what ways are you smart?"*

The Neurobiology of Cognitive Development

The structure and functions of the neurological system are greatly affected by the interaction of infants' experiences and their genetically programmed growth and development. The quality of infants' first relationships with others is very important in early brain growth: it influences thinking, language, and literacy development. Human connections truly shape the neural connections from which infants' minds emerge.

It is the kinds of relationships and emotional communication—especially the early attachment relationships—that affect the brain's biochemistry and wiring: they create the neurological patterns that the child uses to mentally create a view of the world.

> *The brain circuits that hold social and emotional experiences are closely linked to the circuits that create meaning.*

Equally important, researchers now know that emotions also play a very important role in children's attempts to find meaning in their experiences. The brain circuits that hold social and emotional experiences are closely linked to the circuits that create meaning. The way in which infants are held, taken care of, and spoken to; the tone of voice, facial expressions, and eye contact used with them; and even the predictability and timing of responses to their needs—all of these interactions stimulate special parts of the brain.

From these experiences, infants create their first ideas or "opinions" of others, which create important patterns of excitement, evaluation, and response in the brain. These are mental activities that are essential to learning. We now know that it is very difficult to separate emotion, perception, and thinking because they are represented by nearly indistinguishable processes in the brain. Learning does not occur without emotion.

Language and Literacy Development

The toddler period is particularly important for the development of language and vocabulary. Talking, singing, and reading to toddlers appear to increase growth in the left side of the brain, the portion that controls most language functions. Learning parts of speech, differences in sounds, and the meanings of words happens gradually during childhood. However, as toddlers improve their abilities to both understand what others are saying and to express themselves with words, they develop new tools for processing thoughts.

LANGUAGE DEVELOPMENT

Angela awakens from her nap at the child care center. She sits up, rubs her eyes, and says, "Water." Ms. Ruiz fills a cup of water and brings it to her. Angela quickly drinks the water. Ms. Ruiz then allows Angela to play with the empty cup and says, "Water all gone. Angela drank it all up. Is Angela still thirsty?"

In the first few years of life, young children learn (1) that language conveys meaning, (2) the sound system of the language, and (3) the structure of the language system. The above example shows that Angela has learned that language carries meaning and that she can use language to communicate. As children listen to the language used by the people in their lives, they absorb the speech sounds of that language system. Jeremy and Angela will learn to imitate the sounds that are typical of their family, community, and geographic region. As they learn to correctly form sentences, they'll show they're learning the *syntax* (structure) of their language.

It's Saturday, and Bill takes Jeremy with him to run errands. When they return, Ann asks Jeremy, "Where did you eat lunch?"
Jeremy replies, "We eated at McDonald's."

77

Jeremy's reply shows that he's learned how to put words together in a sentence. His use of "eated" shows that he now knows that past-tense words end in -ed. The ability to form such generalizations is an example of young children's amazing cognitive ability. As Jeremy gets older and learns more about the English language, he'll realize there are some exceptions to the general patterns of language, and he'll use *ate* instead of *eated*.

Young children learn the customs and behaviors that go along with communication in the same way that they learn to speak: by participating with others in meaningful interactions, conversations, and shared experiences. Children also learn nonverbal behaviors and conversational techniques through these interactions. For example, in a number of traditional Native American cultures, children are expected to listen while adults speak. Rather than providing opportunities for children to speak, the adults create opportunities for children to listen. Thus, children from some cultural groups view silence as comfortable and expected behavior. Interrupting or speaking too soon after another person has spoken is viewed as rude. In other cultures, children and adults sometimes talk at the same time, and interruptions are acceptable.

Interaction between Thought and Language

Piaget believed that young children's thinking influences the way they use language. He observed that many children under the age of seven often talked to themselves, and he believed that this behavior was evidence of their egocentric thinking. Piaget thought that as children mature cognitively, this behavior of talking to oneself eventually disappears, and social speech develops.

The Russian psychologist Lev Vygotsky believed, however, that young children talk to themselves in order to solve problems or guide their behavior, and that as children get older, their private speech becomes "inner speech"—or thinking in words or sentences. He also believed that in the first few years of life, language and thought develop independently, but that by age two or so, they begin to influence one another. Language—a child's growing vocabulary—improves abstract thinking so that children can use language to process information and better express themselves. These and similar findings show the importance of social interaction and communication in the development of language and cognition in young children.

Vocabulary Development

Young children learn new vocabulary with amazing speed. They learn and remember an average of nine words per day from the beginning of speech until age six. By that time, they will have learned about fourteen thousand words.

Children's first understanding of words is often expanded and refined as they continue to learn about the world. Children improve and expand their vocabulary naturally, for example, as they discover that there are words that sound the same but have different meanings—*son* and *sun*, for example.

> *One of Jeremy's favorite books is Eric Carle's* The Very Hungry Caterpillar. *From this book, Jeremy learned that a caterpillar is a tube-shaped insect that crawls. He was therefore puzzled when he first saw another type of "caterpillar," a toy replica of a Caterpillar-brand tractor.*

By eighteen to twenty months old, children usually have a vocabulary of forty to fifty words. At this time, they begin to form their first sentences, usually made up of two words. It's important to remember that children know more than they are able to say. They often use nonverbal behaviors to further communicate what they mean. The two words *Mommy, sock* could mean either "Mommy's sock," "Mommy, put on my sock," or "Mommy, give me my sock." Context is important for understanding children's true meaning in these early sentences. Between the ages of two and three, toddlers begin to create simple sentences that are close to the correct grammatical structure of their first language.

> *By the time young children are six years old, they will have learned about fourteen thousand words.*

Oral-Language Attempts

As children begin to acquire language, their attempts to copy adult language are full of mistakes. Adults often view young children's developing language as incorrect and believe that it should be corrected. These early language attempts, however, are simply part of their cognitive growth. Soon, toddlers' language will naturally evolve into more accurate forms as they continue to develop cognitively and hear and interact with adult speakers who model correct speech.

Dialects

As anyone who's traveled to various parts of the United States has learned, there are many dialects in our country. Just think about the differences in sounds and pronunciations of the New England area, the Southeast, and the Midwest. The state of Texas alone has five regional dialects. According to linguists, dialects are not lower forms of language; they are simply different forms. All young children learn the dialect of the home and community in which they live.

Bilingualism and Multilingualism

From birth, some children learn two languages simultaneously, and these children truly have two first languages. More and more children in the United States come from homes in which English is not the first language. In addition, many young children are in home, child care, and preschool environments in which different languages are spoken. Scholars who are interested in the language development of bilingual and multilingual children are finding that learning a second language helps both cognitive and linguistic skill development. When matched with children who speak only one language, children who are bilingual outperform them in areas of verbal and nonverbal intellectual measures, analytic reasoning, concept formation, and creativity.

Children learning two languages simultaneously do so at a rapid pace, much as if they were learning only one language. Language development in all cultures is a very natural process, and it is not slowed down in young children who are learning more than one language.

LITERACY DEVELOPMENT

Cheryl has been doing her homework in front of the TV. She takes a break and walks to the kitchen to get something to eat. As she walks back to the living room, she discovers two-year-old Angela scribbling on her notebook. "Angela, that's my homework!" she shouts. Angela looks up at Cheryl and says, "Angela homework."

It's Saturday. Ann's father has come to visit, and the family decides to go to the mall. As they enter the mall, two-year-old Jeremy says, "There's Sears." Ann's father cannot believe his ears. "Jeremy is only two, and he can read Sears," the proud grandfather remarks.

These two situations show that very young children are learning not only about oral language but also about written language. The idea that even very young children are aware of and learning about print is relatively recent.

Interaction among Thought, Language, and Literacy

In the past, teachers, parents, and child development professionals thought that children needed to spend the first five years or so of their lives developing a good foundation in oral language before they could learn to read. After learning the basics of reading, children would then be ready to learn how to write—somewhere around the end of first grade or the beginning of second. Once introduced to writing, young children were expected to produce stories with correct spelling and grammar, good handwriting, and correct punctuation on their first attempt. If they were not successful, their papers and stories were returned to be corrected.

In the 1960s and 1970s, a number of researchers began to question this sequence of reading and writing, or literacy, development. Their research provided new information about how and when young children actually learn to read and write.

Oral language researchers noticed that many young children talked about and were very much interested in print. The two situations above involving Jeremy and Angela are good examples of children's awareness of print.

Reading researchers also saw that some children entered first grade already knowing how to read. While some suspected that these children's parents had taught them how to read, a study found that the parents did not formally teach their young children to read. Instead, these parents did a number of things that seemed to encourage and help early reading behaviors (Durkin 1966):

- They read to their children on a regular basis when the children were quite young.
- They gave their children access to a wide range of printed materials in the home.
- They read and used books, magazines, and newspapers themselves.
- They answered their children's questions about written materials.
- They had writing and drawing tools and paper in the home for their children to use.

Literacy researchers have developed several general ideas about the development of literacy in young children:

- Learning about print begins quite early in life, as early as the first year.
- Young children learn about reading and writing by interacting with others in situations involving print material (sitting in the lap of a parent and being read to, for example).
- Young children develop an awareness of oral and written lan-

guage in a holistic and interrelated way, rather than in a series of steps. In other words, very young children develop ideas about both oral and written language from their environment and while interacting with significant people in their lives in meaningful situations.

- Virtually all children, regardless of socioeconomic background, learn about literacy early in life.

Having positive experiences with oral and written language with others who read and write is a very important key to literacy development. Obviously, child care centers and early child development programs can play a very important role by giving young children positive experiences with books and other written materials.

> *Having positive experiences with oral and written language with others who read and write is a very important key to literacy development.*

Developing Awareness of Print as a Form of Communication

Many young children begin to develop an important new concept as their parents read stories to them: Print has meaning. Researchers now believe that reading aloud to children is the single most important activity for building the understanding and skills that are essential for later reading success. Young children also learn that print has meaning by seeing words in the world around them: on buildings, billboards, restaurant menus, trucks and vans, breakfast cereal boxes, and store products.

Environmental Print. In the story about Jeremy and Sears, how did Jeremy connect the large store at the mall with the letters *S-E-A-R-S* above its door? He had already had a number of experiences that involved both oral and written language. Jeremy had been in the Sears store many times. He was with Bill and Ann when they purchased a new washer and dryer. He watched as the Sears truck arrived and the washer and dryer were delivered and installed. Almost every time Bill and Ann are in Sears, they take Jeremy to the toy department to look around. Jeremy has also heard and seen advertisements for Sears on TV. Together, these experiences helped Jeremy to remember the letters that represent Sears. They are all examples of recognizing *environmental print*.

> *Reading aloud to children is the single most important activity for building the understanding and skills that are essential for later reading success.*

Book Print. For the most part, *book print* differs from environmental print because it usually consists of more than one or two words, has more than one or two lines, and appears in books rather than in the world around a child. Parents, caregivers, and child care professionals all play a critical role in helping young children become aware of books and print. Learning about book print begins at home and in child care centers when parents, older siblings, and other caregivers share books with children. As children hear stories, they begin to get the idea that books can bring them information, pleasure, and comfort. This idea can begin to foster a love of books and independent reading in children.

Reading books at home or in a child care setting gives young children many opportunities to develop literacy skills. Specifically, they learn:

- new information about the world around them
- new vocabulary
- how to take turns talking in conversation (when parents or other caregivers ask questions and children respond)
- the features of print and how to handle books
- the concept of a story

Finally, reading books provides time for parent-child communication. Time spent with books not only helps literacy development, but also promotes positive parent-child interactions.

The Role of Parents and Other Caregivers in Introducing Print. Adult-child interactions in a variety of print situations help children understand that we use printed words in many ways. Parents who actively involve their children in reading environmental print and book print provide them with age-appropriate drawing and writing tools so that they can explore print, and respond to their questions about print help their children make the connection between spoken language and writing.

Print awareness and literacy development depend on children's experiences. As toddlers' first teachers, parents and other caregivers can encourage cognitive, language, and literacy development by exposing very young children to words, concepts, stories, print, and literacy behaviors. More specifically, here are ways parents and caregivers can help:

- Talk with infants and toddlers, sharing everyday events and experiences.
- Name people and things that the child is familiar with, and describe and name events and experiences as they happen.
- Look at picture books together and share stories and other experiences with print.
- Include sounds, rhythms, rhymes, word play, jingles, and songs in daily interactions.
- Provide time to listen to recorded sounds, voices, and music.

- Model reading and other everyday experiences with print-related items (for example, reading books, recipes, news publications; making grocery lists; writing checks, thank-you notes; pointing to signs, billboards; and so on).
- Select and read a variety of age-appropriate story and information books.
- Retell stories of recent experiences in the order they happened: going to the zoo, Mom or Dad washing the car, buying cupcakes for a birthday party, spending the night with grandparents, and so on.

Much is written today about children's "readiness" to learn for pre-kindergarten, kindergarten, and first grade, and table 8.2 shows the types of reading-related knowledge and skills children should have by the end of their third year. Of course, additional developmental steps during ages four through five will be needed before children can actually begin to read.

Table 8.2: **Early Literacy Development (Birth through Age Three)**

• Gain a beginning ability to use language and nonverbal communication
• Recognize that words represent the names of objects, people, and events
• Listen with interest to the spoken word
• Show an ability to both listen and speak
• Continue vocabulary development
• Show an interest in and awareness of sounds and rhythms in speech and music
• Understand the small differences in sounds, rhymes, and rhythms in speech and music
• Enjoy and experiment with spoken sounds and rhythms
• Have an interest in and curiosity about books and book illustrations
• Understand that books have both illustrations and print
• Understand that print represents spoken language
• Understand that print can be used to label, tell a story, and convey a message
• Understand the function of books

- Demonstrate book-handling skills (top/bottom, left/right, front/back orientations; page turning; care, storage, and retrieval)

- Demonstrate awareness of, interest in, and curiosity about environmental print

- Imitate the reading and writing activities of others: look at books, "read" pictures, retell stories, draw and label, imitate writing, try to write letters and numbers, point to words on objects and in books and ask, "What does that say?"

In chapter 8, we focused on the theories of cognitive development. You learned about new ideas regarding toddlers' ability to understand the feelings of others, the multiple intelligences theory, how language develops, the interaction between thinking and language, new ideas about how and when children can learn to read, and the steps you can take to encourage early reading behaviors.

In chapter 9, we'll begin by looking at the biological origins of thinking and language. You'll learn how important good health is for effective learning, and why the way adults respond to toddlers' attempts to speak is so important. During the third year, children begin to act out behaviors and activities that they see others do, and you'll learn why this is another important developmental milestone. Finally, you'll find valuable information on steps you, as a child care professional, can take to help cognitive, language, and literacy development in children ages one through three.

References

Durkin, D. 1966. *Children who read early*. New York: Teachers College Press.

Hughes, M. and M. Donaldson. 1983. The use of hiding games for studying coordination of points. In *Early childhood development and education: Readings in psychology*. Ed. M. Donaldson, R. Grieve, and C. Pratt. New York: Guilford Press.

Factors Influencing Cognitive, Language, and Literacy Development

During children's first three years of rapid brain growth, quality interactions with adults, good physical and mental health care, and rich, stimulating environments will lead to excellent neurological development.

Quality Interactions with Caregivers

Probably at no other time in life is the nature and quality of one's interactions with others as important as it is during early childhood development. This is particularly true for cognitive, language, and literacy development. Children need the following:

- interactions that are positive, helpful, encouraging, and supportive to help build children's self-esteem and self-confidence
- interactions that are thoughtful and logical to help children gain intellectual clarity about their experiences
- interactions that are playful and appropriately humorous to relieve stress and help children think more creatively

ADULT RESPONSES AFFECT LANGUAGE DEVELOPMENT

Studies clearly show that the way adults respond to toddlers' growing language skills is connected to the speed at which speech and reading achievement develop. We have known for many years now that talking, singing, storytelling, and reading to and with children helps their cognitive, language, and literacy development.

When adults encourage children to continue talking about a story or other topic, ask questions, add new information, and substitute new words for familiar ones (such as *scamper* or *dash* for the more familiar word *run*), language development is en-hanced and comprehension is strengthened. This is called the use of *extensions* and *expansions*. Extensions are responses that include the key parts of chil-dren's statements and extend the meaning. For example, Jeremy says, "Get ball." Bill replies, "Oh, you need me to help you get your ball. It rolled under the table." Through this *extension*, Bill tells Jeremy that he understood what he said.

> *Probably at no other time in life is the nature and quality of one's interactions with others as important as it is during early childhood development. This is particularly true for cognitive, language, and literacy development.*

Expansions revise children's original statements, giving children the opportunity to hear the common and correct forms of language. Adults use expansions to give feedback to young children about their use of "overreg-ularizations." For example, Jeremy tells Ann, "We *eated* at McDonald's." She replies, "Oh, you *ate* at McDonald's. What did you have to eat?" She does not *directly* correct Jeremy's "eated," but she responds with the cor-rect verb form and extends it by asking what Jeremy had to eat. Research suggests that adults who use these techniques help children to grow more quickly in their language development and to create more complex sen-tences than children who are around adults who do not use extensions and expansions.

Physical and Mental Health

All learning is improved when children are healthy. At the same time, poor nourishment, inadequate sleep, living with stress, lack of safe and whole-some play, and family conflicts all interfere with learning. Undiagnosed illnesses, developmental delays, emotional disorders, or problems with vi-sion, hearing, or other senses can interfere too.

Again, early diagnosis and intervention is very important, particularly during this time when growth, development, and learning are happening so rapidly. Staff at child care programs and most public schools serving very young children can and should try to link families who need help to community resources such as the public health department, family ser-vices, or other specialized agencies. Programs for low-income families such as Early Head Start and Head Start—which provide physical, dental, psychological, and other assessments as well as enriching age-appropriate learning opportunities—can also help struggling families.

A Rich Play Life

Today, most child development experts believe that play, either with or without toys or other objects, is very important in helping young children develop cognitive, language, and literacy skills. They say that play often involves four steps: exploration, manipulation, practice, and repetition (Garvey 1997). Repetitive play with objects actually helps toddlers learn more about the physical world and develop logical–mathematical thinking. Children between ages one and three often "play" with sounds, syllables, and words, too, which helps language development.

A rich play life in infancy and early childhood builds the bridge to language, learning, literacy, and later academic success.

During children's third year, *sociodramatic* play begins. In sociodramatic play, toddlers begin to imitate what they have seen others, usually adults or older children, do. Three-year-olds' sociodramatic play usually has no organized theme or plot. Play at this age often involves collecting, hauling, carrying, and dumping objects. Children tend to repeat play over and over. Jeremy's playing "garbage collection" is a perfect example. At this age children act out the basics or essentials of certain patterns that they are familiar with, such as eating a meal, visiting the doctor, or picking up trash.

Playing alone or with others is essential to child development. Play with toys or other play objects that are *open-ended* allows toddlers to create concepts, meaning, and ideas that are very interesting to them—and give toddlers the essential support for early cognitive, language, and literacy development. Unlike toys that have limited use or that can be used in only one way, open-ended toys and playthings can be used in many different ways and with different levels of skill. Blocks, a good example of open-ended play objects, can be stacked, loaded in a wagon, used to build a tower, clapped to music, or used to represent a person, vehicle, animal, or railroad track.

Blocks are enjoyed differently at different ages as toddlers' play and abilities change over time. Blocks have an enduring quality essential to play that helps cognitive and language development at all ages. In contrast, a wind-up mechanical or electronic toy is of little value if all the child can do with it is watch it "perform," or if its use requires adult assistance.

Unlike toys that have limited use or that can be used in only one way, open-ended toys and playthings can be used in many different ways and with different levels of skill.

While the social interaction skills of toddlers are awkward and unsophisticated, older toddlers benefit from opportunities to interact with other children in spontaneous and unstructured pretend play. Through these opportunities, children gain language and social interaction skills. A rich play life in infancy and early childhood builds the bridge to language, learning, literacy, and later academic success.

Reference

Garvey, C. 1977. *Play*. Cambridge, Mass.: Harvard University Press.

The Role of the Early Childhood Professional

1. Acknowledge that each child is unique in his cognitive, language, and literacy development.
2. Respect sociocultural, linguistic, and socioeconomic differences among young children and their families.
3. Identify cognitive, language, and literacy needs in young children that may require special attention, services, or programs.
4. Understand that young children process information differently than older children and adults.
5. Provide safe and enriched environments so that young children can explore freely.
6. Provide a variety of interesting materials to promote thinking, talking, drawing, reading, and writing.
7. Provide opportunities for young children to interact, talk, read, draw, and write with other children and adults.
8. Demonstrate interest in, and curiosity about, the world.
9. Use engaging oral language with children and model the uses of writing and print in many meaningful contexts.
10. Respond in a timely manner to children's need for scaffolding to help them grasp a concept or engage in a new skill.

Discussion Questions

1. The next time a toddler in your program shares a particular fear with you, try inviting her (and perhaps the other toddlers in the program too) to come up with a way to solve the problem to alleviate the fear. For example, if a toddler is afraid a ghost is hiding in your bathroom, and therefore does not want to use the bathroom, ask her and the other toddlers how they might get rid of the ghost. If the toddlers are having trouble coming up with solutions, make some suggestions to get them started. For example, ask them, "Should we hang a sign on the bathroom door that says, 'No ghosts allowed?'" or "Should we spray some special 'ghost-be-gone' potion into the bathroom?" (using a spray bottle filled with tap water).
2. Using Gardner's multiple intelligences theory, create a special page about each toddler in your care, identifying individual strengths and weaknesses. Are there any trends in the group as a whole? How might you adjust your curriculum to play to the strong points of the group while strengthening the weaknesses?
3. What activities and materials do you currently include in your program that encourage an interest in reading and writing? Based on the current research on literacy development discussed in chapter 8, are there activities or materials you could add to your setting that might strengthen

the children's awareness of oral and written language? Try implementing one new activity in your setting, and then monitor its impact. For example, after you read a book aloud, invite toddlers to participate in a question-and-answer session about the book. Or, if you don't have a writing center readily available, set up an area with writing and drawing tools that the children can use whenever they're interested.

Further Reading

Brazelton, T. B., and M. D. Greenspan. 2000. *The irreducible needs of children: What every child must have to grow, learn, and flourish.* Cambridge, Mass.: Perseus Books.

Gardner, H. 1999. *Intelligence reframed: Multiple intelligences for the 21st century.* New York: Basic Books.

Greenspan, S. I., and S. Wieder. 1997. *The child with special needs: Encouraging intellectual and emotional growth.* New York: Perseus Books.

McMullen, M. B. 1999. "Research in review: Achieving best practices in infant and toddler care and education." *Young children* 54:4, 69–76.

Rideout, V. I., E. A. Vanderwater, and E. A. Wartella. 2003. *Zero to six: Electronic media in the lives of infants, toddlers, and preschoolers.* Menlo Park, Calif.: Henry J. Kaiser Family Foundation.

Samway, K. D., and D. McKeon. 1999. *Myths and realities: Best practices for language minority students.* Portsmouth, N.H.: Heinemann.

Singer, D. G., and J. L. Singer. 2001. *Make-believe games and activities for imaginative play: A book for parents, teachers, and the young children in their lives.* Washington, D.C.: American Psychological Association.

Other Resources

• National Center for Children in Poverty (NCCP). 2002. "Promoting the well-being of infants, toddlers, and their families: Innovative community and state strategies." www.nccp.org.

• National Head Start Association. www.nhsa.org.

Index

Other Resources from 🍁 Redleaf Press